Film Noir Style

Film Noir Style

The Killer 1940s

Kimberly Truhler

GoodKnight Books
Pittsburgh, Pennsylvania

GoodKnight Books

© 2020 by Kimberly Truhler

Published by GoodKnight Books, Pittsburgh, Pennsylvania.

Printed in the United States of America.

ISBN 9781732273597

Library of Congress Control Number: 2020940953

Cover photo of Ava Gardner, back cover photo of Orson Welles and Rita Hayworth, and frontispiece photo of Rita Hayworth all from the Everett Collection.

For Kevin
The best person I have ever known

Contents

The Year of Transition
1946

The Post-War Years
1947—1950

Louise Brooks leads many men astray as the intrigante Lulu in *Pandora's Box*. (Everett Collection)

Introduction

Style is everywhere in the world of film noir. Yes, the genre explores the dark side of human nature, centering on sins like lust and greed and on crimes ranging from robbery to murder. At the same time, many of the movies are sexy and stunningly beautiful. This book celebrates the many artists involved in their production. The spotlight, however, is on the costumes and their designers who too often are left out of the conversation. This omission is shocking considering that the words "film noir" so easily evoke images of strong women who are elegantly understated by day and dangerously glamorous by night. Or maybe "noir" conjures scenes of hard-boiled detectives and world-weary men in suits and trench coats trying to find their way in an America troubled by war.

Costume designers helped define the look of noir and did it so well that their influence lives on in both film and fashion, where many costumes have become iconic. This accomplishment is impressive considering that the bulk of these movies were not big-budget hits, the designs faced challenges from rationing during the war to pressure from the Motion Picture Production Code, and each studio had its own style voice and team of designers.

As a genre, film noir is different from any other. Unlike westerns or musicals, film noir was termed almost after the fact by French film critics in the mid-1940s. They observed a darker mood in American cinema that emerged during the decade and would continue into the 1950s.

Much of this mood grew from the advent of World War II. Studios started to turn to the tough crime fiction of authors such as James M. Cain, Dashiell Hammett, and Raymond Chandler as source material for their scripts. Screenwriters created appealing anti-heroes who blurred the lines between good and bad. Women were strong characters in the world of noir, often equal

The German Expressionist film *The Cabinet of Dr. Caligari* (1920) was influential on noir, especially *The Lady from Shanghai* (1947). (Everett Collection)

to the men, reflecting changing roles during the war especially in the workforce.

In many cases the directors and cinematographers were émigrés who had fled Eastern Europe during the rise of Nazism. Not only did their artistic vision help shape the look of noir, their suffering and alienation brought even more realism to the genre. As a result, the two types of movies that would make up film noir—crime thrillers and murder dramas—stood in sharp contrast to the romantic fantasies of earlier decades and reflected that it was hard, if not impossible, for many to achieve the American dream.

Some of film noir's strongest cinematic influences are found in 1920s German Expressionism. That movement had its origins in the anger, betrayal, and isolation that Germany experienced as a result of World War I. The country's mood was reflected in the style of the movies, from scenes shot at odd angles to dramatic cinematography that often was filled with more shadows than light. They also featured seductive intrigantes—women who intrigue—predecessors to the even more dangerous femmes fatales. Their stories were told with a frank portrayal of sexuality that Hollywood's Production Code would soon outlaw.

UFA, Germany's film production company, was a source of motion pictures that would inspire noir, such as Robert Wiene's *The Cabinet of Dr. Caligari* (1920), F.W. Murnau's *Nosferatu* (1922), Fritz Lang's *Metropolis* (1927) and *M* (1931), G.W. Pabst's *Pandora's Box* (1929), and Josef von Sternberg's international hit, *The Blue Angel* (1930). Many directors who spent time at UFA would create some of the best of noir. Fritz Lang made *The Big Heat* (1953), Sternberg did *The Shanghai Gesture* (1941), Robert Siodmak directed *The Killers* (1946), Michael Curtiz did *Mildred Pierce* (1945), and Alfred Hitchcock made *Notorious* (1946). Still more European émigrés contributed to film noir once they started working in Hollywood, such as Otto Preminger, who directed *Laura* (1944), and Billy Wilder, who made *Double Indemnity* (1944).

Inspiration for film noir would come from America as well, especially in the years before the Production Code took effect. Pre-Code gangster pictures like William Wellman's *The Public Enemy* (1931) and Howard Hawks' *Scarface* (1932) featured violent criminals as their main characters. It was the dawn of the anti-hero. In addition, horror films of the pre-Code era, such as Tod Browning's *Dracula* and James Whale's *Frankenstein* (both 1931), helped to set the noir mood, especially the extraordinary darkness created by their cinematographers Karl Freund and Arthur Edeson, the latter of whom would later photograph *The Maltese Falcon* (1941).

Sternberg was another source of proto-noir once he started working in America. His renowned visual style, created with cinematographer Lee Garmes, included filtering light through venetian blinds. He also made a model intrigante of Marlene Dietrich in *Morocco* (1930) and especially in *Shanghai Express* (1932). His muse would influence many women in noir, from Lauren Bacall in *To Have and Have Not* (1944) to Lizabeth Scott in *Dead Reckoning* (1947).

The entry of the United States into World War II affected both the story lines and the costumes of film noir. The trench coat, which became a staple of the genre, had its origins in men's military uniforms. For practical purposes, this outerwear often became part of a veteran's wardrobe once he returned home. But the biggest impact on 1940s style came as a result of nationwide rationing during the war, which stipulated what types of fabric could be used and, perhaps more important, how much fabric could be used. In March 1942 the War Production Board issued Limitation Order 85 to maximize the amount of cloth available for military use. L-85 was a strict set of rules and restrictions for the garment industry and civilian fashion. For example, the order dictated the maximum length and circumference of skirts and dresses. It also controlled the amount of detail in a design, whether it be pockets, pleating, collars, ruffles, bows, or buttons.

Although Hollywood costume design departments had a number of resources at their disposal, they were charged with supporting and inspiring audiences affected by government regulations. This obligation resulted in the more austere aesthetic of the decade and manifested itself in pieces such as the pencil skirt, which became a signature style of women in film noir. It also put

Marlene Dietrich as Josef von Sternberg's model intrigante in the pre-Code *Shanghai Express*. (Everett Collection)

an emphasis on form and fit, which can be seen in suiting and dresses. In addition, the Production Code, which prevented any outfit from revealing too much, made costume designers cautious yet creative when working sensuality into the era's evening gowns.

Each studio and its team of designers made contributions to the style of film noir. Although discussion has yet to abate concerning which movies should be labeled as noir—and this book will explore some of that controversy—one title not subject to argument and often credited as the first film noir is Warner Bros.' *The Maltese Falcon*. The costume design is by Orry-Kelly, who was then head of the department and worked with star Humphrey Bogart to establish the look of Dashiell Hammett's private eye, Sam Spade. Warner Bros. became renowned for noir, and its costume designers Orry-Kelly, Milo Anderson, and Leah Rhodes were so in sync, they seemed to work as one. They helped define the studio's style voice as well as that of noir itself, creating costumes for essential pictures in the genre, including those that co-starred Bogart and Lauren Bacall. Anderson designed the costumes for their first film together, *To Have and Have Not*, and Rhodes was responsible for the couple's other classics, *The Big Sleep* (1946) and *Key Largo* (1948). The suiting that defined the decade along with the seemingly ever-present shoulder pads can be seen in Anderson's costumes for Joan Crawford in *Mildred Pierce*.

Like Warner Bros., RKO became known for some of the grittier film noir in Hollywood. Its costume designers may be less recognizable by name, but RKO's department head Edward Stevenson was behind the powerful proto-noir *Citizen Kane* (1941) and celebrated for his costumes in the films noir *Murder, My Sweet* (1944) and *Out of the Past* (1947). He is perhaps best known for the latter, skillfully using wardrobe to illustrate Jane Greer's double-edged personality. RKO also assigned costume designer Renié to several noir productions, including classics such as *Crack-Up* (1946) and *Riff-Raff* (1947) the following year. In 1981 she would come back to her roots when she worked on Lawrence Kasdan's neo-noir *Body Heat*. Alfred Hitchcock's *Notorious* (1946) was another noir that technically came from RKO, although Ingrid Bergman had enough star power to request that Paramount's Edith Head design the costumes.

In contrast to Warner Bros. and RKO, Paramount was known for its polish and sophistication. Even so, the studio made significant contributions to film noir. Edith Head directed the costume design department during the era and had ongoing partnerships with directors and actresses, including Billy Wilder and Head's close friend Barbara Stanwyck. They all worked together in the picture that is often considered the quintessential film noir, *Double Indemnity*. The seductive anklet Stanwyck sports was just the start of Head's memorable costume design in the production.

Head and Wilder would work together again on another noir giant, *Sunset Boulevard* (1950), a project Edith relished in particular because it meant dressing its star, Gloria Swanson. Head would work her magic on another Paramount star, Veronica Lake, establishing her style in three films with Alan Ladd—*This Gun for Hire* and *The Glass Key* (both 1942), and *The Blue Dahlia* (1946).

Pre-Code horror films like *Dracula* (1931) inspired some of the mood of noir. (Greenbriar Collection)

Columbia is known for its share of films noir, especially those starring sultry screen goddess Rita Hayworth. *Gilda* (1946) and *The Lady from Shanghai* (1947) are two greats in the film noir genre, and both feature costume design by department head Jean Louis. *Gilda* includes a cavalcade of sensual gowns that show the glamour of the era while also dancing around the Production Code. Louis went on to design for Columbia noir of the 1950s, including two that co-star Gloria Grahame and Glenn Ford, *The Big Heat* and *Human Desire* (1954).

Like Louis, Universal's head of costume design Vera West made a huge

Ann Dvorak in *Scarface* (1932) exudes the attitude that would be identified with the tough women of film noir. (Everett Collection)

impact with her vision of a femme fatale for one of Hollywood's most popular actresses. West was best known for her "horror couture" in movies like *The Bride of Frankenstein* (1935), where she was uncredited. She put all that aside when MGM loaned Ava Gardner to Universal to star in *The Killers*. Gardner's costumes range from seductive gowns to accessible everyday pieces, such as a simple blouse and skirt, and include a twist on an archetypal noir costume. During West's tenure Universal tapped into other talented costume designers who would continue after she retired. That diversity is evident in a range of films noir from the studio, such as *Scarlet Street* (1945) with design by Travis Banton; *Criss Cross* (1949) with design by Yvonne Wood; and *Touch of Evil* (1958) with design by Bill Thomas.

Grit meshed with glamour at 20th Century Fox. One of its top costume designers, Bonnie Cashin, came straight from the fashion world. She worked multiple times with director Otto Preminger, including designing a stylish haute couture wardrobe for Gene Tierney in *Laura*. Cashin also created costumes for Fox stars Alice Faye and Linda Darnell in *Fallen Angel* (1945) and for Joan Blondell and Coleen Gray in *Nightmare Alley* (1947). Gwen Wakeling, the studio's early head of costume design, established the style of Carole Landis and Betty Grable in Fox's first film noir, *I Wake Up Screaming* (1941). When Charles LeMaire took over the department in 1942, he became known for even more noir, including maintaining Joan Crawford's strong-shouldered look in *Daisy Kenyon* (1947).

Even MGM, a studio known for family fare like the Andy Hardy series and glitzy musicals, took a turn toward the dark side and plunged into film noir. *Lady in the Lake* (1947), with design by Irene, and *Act of Violence* (1949) and *The Asphalt Jungle* (1950), both with design by Helen Rose, came from MGM. The best-known noir from the studio is *The Postman Always Rings Twice* (1946), thanks to its sensual star Lana Turner. Irene was head of costume design and dressed the femme fatale in a nearly all-white wardrobe with precise motives in mind. Thanks to those costumes, Turner enjoyed one of the all-time great movie entrances.

The costumes of film noir helped to define the style of the 1940s. The designs reflected the global struggles and austerity associated with World War II. Studio designers had access to many resources to dress their stars, but that was not the audience's reality. Costumes ranged from the simplicity of a sweater and skirt in a movie like *The Killers* to the smart suiting in *The Big Sleep* to the aspirational glamour of *Gilda*'s gowns. All three are 1946 pictures—arguably the greatest year of film noir costume design because of the films' ongoing influence on fashion. Others from that year include *The Postman Always Rings Twice*, *The Blue Dahlia*, and *Notorious*.

While most of the crime thrillers and murder dramas that make up film noir were not A-list productions, they are among the most recognized and applauded movies of the era thanks largely to the style that made them famous.

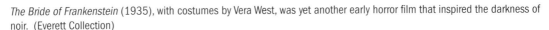

The Bride of Frankenstein (1935), with costumes by Vera West, was yet another early horror film that inspired the darkness of noir. (Everett Collection)

Before the War
1940—1941

Actress Kathryn Adams models a gold wool coat, straw hat, and kid gloves in 1940. (Everett Collection)

From Depression to War

From the moment the 1940s began, much of the world was at war.

On September 3, 1939, Great Britain and France declared war on Germany after Adolf Hitler invaded Poland days earlier. Although the United States was not yet sending troops, a debate had begun between those who believed in the isolationist stance the country had taken since World War I and those who wanted to join in the fight. America had already been in the midst of another kind of battle at home.

For the entirety of the 1930s, the country had been ravaged by the Great Depression. People lost their homes, their savings, and then even their ability to work when business after business shut down. Unemployment reached a peak of 24.9 percent in 1933 and would remain around 20 percent for half the decade.

Rather than reflect the reality of suffering during the Depression, Hollywood chose to offer escape. The theaters became a physical escape; for around twenty-five cents, people could spend hours at the movies. The films became an emotional escape, filled with aspirational fantasies of people drinking, dancing, and romancing in the most glamorous of surroundings—shop girls who made good and found fortune (and happiness?) with wealthy husbands, and socialites who stayed and played in penthouses decorated entirely in white. None of the characters seemed to have a care in the world. *Top Hat* (1935) and other sophisticated musical comedies like those starring Fred Astaire and Ginger Rogers were the perfect salve for the decade's sorrows.

Often considered the greatest year in film history for the quantity and quality of pictures that premiered, 1939 saw the releases of *Gone With the Wind*, *The Wizard of Oz*, *Wuthering Heights*, *The Women*, and on and on. *Confessions of a Nazi Spy* also premiered that year, showing that America did indeed have war with Germany on its collective mind.

The United States would not officially declare war until Japan attacked Pearl Harbor in December 1941, but military spending had already started by 1940. It was an effort to supply the allies with matériel and to prepare the country for conflict looming on the horizon. The spending from the mobilization would mark America's emergence from the Great Depression and debut as a global superpower.

Gearing up for war helped bring unemployment down to 14.6 percent in 1940 (from 17.2 percent the previous year) with 12 million women as part of the overall workforce. However, as historian Allan Winkler describes: "Women were without question sec-

Women deciding on their vacation destination in January 1940; those plans would soon be impossible because of the war. (Everett Collection)

ond-class citizens at the start of the conflict. They were particularly conscious of discrimination in the labor market. Numerous jobs were simply closed to them, which led to a concentration of working women in retail trade and domestic service. In those jobs they did hold, women usually received smaller paychecks than men. During the Great Depression, conditions had worsened as … [women] confronted jobless men who keenly resented the new competition."

By the time World War II began, the number of women in the workforce had already climbed to 14.6 million. This number would keep climbing as it became clear that women were needed to help win the war. Their lives would change considerably in the coming years. And their style would change considerably as well.

The fall of Paris in June 1940 had an immediate impact on the fashion industry. Luxurious raw materials such as silk could no longer be exported from Europe. And although many French couturiers managed to stay open—around sixty continued selling to Germans and German collaborators—they no longer had customers or even publicity abroad.

Great Britain and the United States started looking to their own designers to supply inspiration. Although many people considered Paris as the fashion center of the world, Hollywood had been leading the way since the 1930s. For starters, the studios in Hollywood had an enormous captive audience. In 1930 at the beginning of the Depression, "weekly cinema attendance was 80 million people, approximately 65 percent of the resident U.S. population," according to political scientist Dr. Michelle Pautz.

Consider the talent Hollywood had to offer. MGM's head costume designer Adrian established the style of Greta Garbo, Joan Crawford, and Jean Harlow. Paramount's head costume designer Travis Banton did the same with Marlene Dietrich, Carole Lombard, and Kay Francis. The sway that Hollywood had over style is unsurprising considering how many heads of costume design departments—Banton, Howard Greer (Paramount), Robert Kalloch (Columbia), and Bernard Newman (RKO)—originally came from the world of couture. Signs of their dominance

Since numerous jobs were off-limits before the war, women tended to work in domestic service and retail. (Both photos, Everett Collection)

Adrian's gown for Joan Crawford in *Letty Lynton* was one of the most influential costumes of the 1930s. Its design was in stark contrast to those in the austere 1940s. (GKB Collection)

were everywhere: in newspaper articles, gossip columns, movie magazines, apparel awards, and fashion trends. Not only did their designs trickle into mainstream fashion, but department stores also sold copies of popular costumes and film-capsule collections. Macy's "Cinema Shop," for example, was but one place customers could find copies of Crawford's white organdy gown from 1932's *Letty Lynton*. Audiences longed to emulate the fashions of their favorite stars, especially the sensual, body-conscious, bias-cut gowns that were all over the screen during the Art Deco era.

The costumes in film noir from before the war show the evolution from 1930s to 1940s style.

In both *I Wake Up Screaming* and *The Shanghai Gesture*, the figure-hugging gowns still reflect the long and lean silhouette of the 1930s. Luxurious fabrics like satin and chiffon and adornments like lace and shimmering sequins are seen in numerous costumes in these early films noir. Many of these features would not be practical or even possible for women once the war began.

Of the three pre-war films noir featured in this book, *The Maltese Falcon* comes closest in look to what 1940s style would become. Adrian had already been developing a stronger shoulder line for Garbo and Crawford in the 1930s, and Orry-Kelly incorporated it into many of Mary Astor's costumes. That design detail would get stronger still during the war years.

The films noir that premiered in 1941 signaled a serious mood in Hollywood and in all of America. They also featured stronger and more independent women, seen in the intrigantes and the more lethal femmes fatales who helped define the genre with both attitude and style. It was only the beginning; there was much more to come.

Hollywood costume designers at a 1941 fashion show: (standing) Orry-Kelly, Travis Banton, and Adrian and (seated) Bernard Newman, Edith Head, and Irene. (Author Collection)

Fashionable femme fatale Brigid O'Shaughnessy hires and seduces Sam Spade. (Everett Collection)

The Maltese Falcon

Premiere: October 3, 1941
Director: John Huston
Costume designer: Orry-Kelly
Studio: Warner Bros.

This is where it all began.

In 1930 Dashiell Hammett, a former operative for the Pinkerton National Detective Agency, wrote the perfect book to launch the genre of film noir. Set in the streets of San Francisco, *The Maltese Falcon* described a world he knew well—violent, avaricious, and cold. No one was honest. What made his fiction different was that his hero, private investigator Sam Spade, embodied those characteristics as much as the criminals, while living by his own moral code. There was real brutality among the thieves, and Spade both delivered blows and suffered them as he navigated the case.

Aspiring filmmaker John Huston, then in his mid-thirties, saw the cinema in Hammett's story and chose *The Maltese Falcon* to be his first directorial project. Working at Warner Bros., the studio that had cornered the market on gangster pictures, Huston captured the mood of noir from the very start of the picture. A sinister statue of a black bird drenched in darkness. The ghostly reveal of the opening credits. The legend of the Falcon scrolling on-screen. Then a segue to a gray San Francisco day outside the office of Spade and Archer. And the man sitting at Spade's desk and rolling a cigarette is Humphrey Bogart.

There had been plenty of inspirational predecessors to *The Maltese Falcon*. The style and dramatic lighting of German Expressionism were particularly influential, from films like Fritz Lang's *Metropolis* and *M*, and Josef von Sternberg's *The Blue Angel* and *Shanghai Express*. The violent criminals who were central characters in pre-Code gangster films like *The Public Enemy* and *Scarface* were more interesting than any on the right side of the law. Early attempts at capturing Dashiell Hammett's work on film included *The Thin Man* (1934) and *The Glass Key* (1935).

In the office of Spade and Archer, Brigid's beauty and respectable style distract Miles Archer from imminent danger. (GKB Collection)

Even *The Maltese Falcon* had been produced twice, in a 1931 version starring Ricardo Cortez and then again five years later with the loosely based *Satan Met a Lady* (1936) with Warren William. Neither captured the novel's brilliance. It took John Huston to make it a classic.

Huston had spent the late 1930s writing screenplays for some of Warners' biggest hits and brought a simple approach to his version of *The Maltese Falcon*: He decided to follow the plot of the book instead of trying to insert his own artistic interpretation, as had other directors and screenwriters. Huston used Hammett's novel as a road map and even storyboarded each scene, right down to the camera moves. This proved critical, especially when shooting the final scenes in Spade's apartment. Rather than doing a series of cuts, he and cinematographer Arthur Edeson worked out every moment in the seven-minute scene to include all the main characters—twenty-two complicated, uninterrupted moves that were purely cinematic. It was something that had never before been attempted in film.

Huston's commitment to Hammett's story was matched by Edeson's lighting, which established the look of *The Maltese Falcon*. German Expressionism influenced Edeson and his work, especially the dramatic lighting he created for *Frankenstein*, and it inspired the look of all film noir to follow. In Huston's *The Maltese Falcon* Edeson constructed a world in which characters live practically in the dark. Scenes often take place at night in dimly lit streets, office buildings, or rooms where criminals reside. The characters feel closed in. To accomplish this, Huston defied convention and built his sets with ceilings, and Edeson relied on lamps rather than overhead studio lighting to more closely mirror real life.

Bogart biographers A.M. Sperber and Eric Lax said, "Eliminating overhead lights in favor of natural lighting imparted both a gritty realism and a sense of claustrophobia in a story played out mostly in oppressive interiors."

A commitment by Huston and Edeson to use the camera to tell the story also proved groundbreaking. They employed inventive camera angles, such as shots from the floor up to show the imposing size of Kasper Gutman, played by Sydney Greenstreet. And because the book told the story from Spade's perspective, so did the movie. Aside from witnessing the murder of Miles

Spade finds himself in close-quarters combat with the sinister Kasper Gutman. (Everett Collection)

Archer (Jerome Cowan) in the first reel, the audience learns and experiences everything right along with Spade.

The audience becomes a part of the detective's world, going with Spade when he works and where he lives. His apartment sets a standard in 1940s film noir style. Highly masculine and sparsely decorated, the small studio stands in sharp contrast to the grand Art Deco penthouses of 1930s films. Photos of race horses decorate the mantle. Leather club chairs, a desk, and a bed dominate the room, which serves as both a sitting and sleeping area. When the police telephone at one o'clock in the morning, Spade takes the call lying in the dark. The camera lingers on his bedside table, which includes a silver alarm clock sitting on a book, an ashtray and tobacco tossed on top of a newspaper, and a bottle of whiskey stashed below. Film critic Richard Schickel described Sam Spade's lifestyle as possessing "that special kind of unshaven squalor that is the mark of bachelorhood in a modern American city." This is Spade's private place, although people go in and out all the time. The small apartment nearly bursts at the seams when all the crooks invade at the end of the movie.

Style permeates the production, from the direction, cinematography, and set design to the costume design of Orry-Kelly. At this time Orry-Kelly, known to his friends as Jack, had been

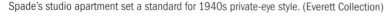

Spade's studio apartment set a standard for 1940s private-eye style. (Everett Collection)

in charge of the Warner Bros. costume design department for nearly a decade and was central to establishing the studio's style voice. His journey to Hollywood had been different from that of his contemporaries, such as Adrian at MGM and Travis Banton at Paramount.

Orry-Kelly was born in Australia and originally sought to be an actor. Holding on to that dream, he moved to New York City in 1921 and became friends and roommates with another struggling actor, Archibald Leach. Orry-Kelly went to work in the theater, transitioning from acting to set decoration to costume design. There he found his true talent and soon began creating costumes for Broadway stars like Ethel Barrymore and Katharine Hepburn. Meanwhile, Archie Leach had found his own success in Hollywood as Cary Grant and encouraged his friend Jack to join him there. Convinced of his talent, Orry-Kelly traveled to California and another Jack—Jack L. Warner—made him head of the Warner Bros. costume design department in 1932.

Orry-Kelly became known for setting the style of many actresses, from Kay Francis to Ann Sheridan to Bette Davis. He added leading lady Mary Astor to the list when she jumped at the chance to act in *The Maltese Falcon* because of what she called Huston's "humdinger" of a script. Astor was a twenty-year screen veteran who had played good girls in movies like *Dodsworth* (1936) and would become known for mother roles at MGM in pictures like *Meet Me in St. Louis* (1944) and others. In *The Maltese Falcon* she proved she was also very good at being bad.

Above: Orry-Kelly discusses costume design for *City for Conquest* (1940) with Ann Sheridan. (Everett Collection) Below: Director John Huston (left) with Peter Lorre, Mary Astor, and Humphrey Bogart. (GKB Collection)

John Huston saw Mary Astor's potential as a femme fatale after a real-life scandal erupted in 1936 around her affair with playwright George S. Kaufman, which she documented in a diary that became public. Huston script girl Meta Carpenter described Astor as "a hard-edged beauty with an aura of worldliness after the headline stories." The salacious details that emerged during the divorce trial gave Astor a certain edge and glamour that were perfect for the character of Brigid O'Shaughnessy.

Astor captured the many facets of this complicated femme fatale with Orry-Kelly's help. In her memoir, *A Life on Film*, Astor wrote that she found her character "attractive, charming, appealingly feminine and helpless, and a complete liar and murderess." Violence is part of Brigid's character. In one exchange, she slaps, kicks, and pistol-whips Peter Lorre's character, Joel Cairo. In another, she shoots the private eye's partner at point-blank range.

Orry-Kelly knew that Astor's ladylike wardrobe would be a weapon that helps her character

Orry-Kelly was known for his love of winged collars and blouses without buttons. This ladylike ensemble features both. (Everett Collection)

A time of transition: Astor still sports the shingle haircut of the 1930s while wearing a striped, strong-shouldered robe that's pure 1940s style. (GKB Collection)

hide her crimes. Her relatively conservative costumes and style in *The Maltese Falcon* also show a transition in fashion from the 1930s to 1940s. Astor's shingle haircut, a version of the bob cut very short, is an example of a style that had become popular in the Art Deco era. In *The Maltese Falcon*, her hair is tidy and tight, still incorporating the controlled waves of the 1930s. In the 1940s, especially in film noir, hair would get longer and looser on stars like Veronica Lake, Rita Hayworth, and Ava Gardner.

Some of Astor's accessories—such as the fox stole worn in the character's introduction—are also associated more with the 1930s. However, most of her costumes step firmly into the 1940s, each calculated to obtain Spade's allegiance. Brigid meets him in a respectable two-tone tailored suit. She welcomes him to her hotel room in a striped robe. A snug pencil skirt and blouse adorned with a flower later elicit a kiss from the detective, and broad-shouldered fur coats show her strength in tense moments. Her look establishes the prototypical femme fatale wardrobe

Bogart was responsible for his own iconic style—his wardrobe came straight from his own closet. (Everett Collection)

for the genre. Even so, the memorable style from *The Maltese Falcon* isn't Astor's—it's Bogart's.

Humphrey Bogart had spent years playing supporting parts at Warner Bros., many of them gangsters. A shift started with *High Sierra* (1941) from a screenplay by Huston. Bogart enacted a gangster once again, but this time as the leading man. *The Maltese Falcon* followed and it changed his career forever—one of those times in Hollywood history when an actor is perfectly matched with a role. In this case the match went even further; not only did Bogart become Spade, but Spade would become Bogart.

Dashiell Hammett's description of the private eye didn't resemble the actor. "He looked rather pleasantly like a blonde satan," wrote Hammett of Spade in the book. Yet Bogart would make the character his own. He was at a point in his life and career where he had plenty of experience, including a volatile and often violent marriage, and all of it helped him capture the moral ambiguity of Sam Spade. In *The New Yorker* Pauline Kael described the character as a "mixture of avarice and honor, sexuality and fear." There's an intensity about Bogart's portrayal of the detective, how he studies each of the thieves as they're speaking to him. Spade would become such a part of the Bogart persona that he played this kind of character again and again throughout his career.

Spade's clothes helped to define his character. In contrast to Astor's custom-made costumes, Spade's clothes came straight from Bogart's own closet. This was a common practice at Warner Bros. to keep costs down. In his first scene the detective sports a dark, double-breasted chalk-stripe suit, which would become something of a uniform for Bogart. Later he wears a black, single-breasted three-piece suit and often looks slightly rumpled due to a shirt collar that refuses to lie flat. He keeps his keys on a chain connected to his belt loop, an accessory repeated five years later when Bogart plays Philip Marlowe in *The Big Sleep*. Spade pairs all outfits with a fedora when he goes out, which becomes another part of his signature style. And on cold foggy nights, he puts on a black, double-breasted overcoat that would evolve into the memorable trench coat seen in the last reel of *Casablanca* (1942). With the character of Sam Spade, Bogart began to control the legacy of his style.

The Maltese Falcon proved a milestone in cinema in everything from the direction, lighting, and production design to the costumes. Orry-Kelly's wardrobe for Mary Astor set a precedent for femmes fatales who used ladylike clothes to hide their intentions and seduce through suggestion. Humphrey Bogart, with clothes from his own closet, laid out the uniform for many film noir heroes to come, including his own character of Philip Marlowe in *The Big Sleep*. Bogart's style, attitude, and masculinity gave America a needed role model as another world war approached.

The Maltese Falcon, a film filled with darkness, continues to be celebrated for its definitive characters and classic lines of dialogue. John Huston credits Bogart—inspired by Shakespeare's *The Tempest* and channeling the character of Spade—for the film's famous closing line. Spade describes the value of the black bird as "the stuff that dreams are made of." The same could be said of *The Maltese Falcon* and its impact on the genre of film noir.

Betty Grable's pin-striped suit is a perfect example of early 1940s style and one of many influential suits from film noir. (Everett Collection)

I Wake Up Screaming

Premiere: November 14, 1941
Director: H. Bruce Humberstone
Costume designer: Gwen Wakeling
Studio: 20th Century Fox

I Wake Up Screaming, based on Steve Fisher's novel of the same name, is a story of sexual obsession and murder that also comments on the dark side of becoming a star. Director Bruce Humberstone made the book into a remarkable film noir, all the more notable for its relative obscurity. This first film noir from 20th Century Fox premiered only a month after *The Maltese Falcon* and helped establish many standards of the genre—a story told in flashback, characters hidden in shadow, scenes shot from odd angles to create mood, and dramatic cinematography with light filtered through blinds.

Style is at the very center of *I Wake Up Screaming*, and head costume designer Gwen Wakeling had the challenge of creating wardrobes for two rising Fox stars, Carole Landis and Betty Grable. As Vicky Lynn, Landis is an intrigante who seduces in every ensemble she wears. As Vicky's sister Jill, Grable is the all-American good girl whose style evolves through her journey from wide-eyed innocent to woman in love. Their costumes show the transition from 1930s to 1940s style as well as the overall mien of film noir.

The look of noir is present from the beginning of *I Wake Up Screaming*. Victor Mature plays Frankie Christopher, a promoter of everything from prizefighters to fan dancers. Frankie is suspected of murder and seen under hot lights at a police station. Throughout the picture, the direction of Bruce Humberstone and the cinematography of Edward Cronjager are stunning—light through the window diffused by cigarette smoke; shadows of the interrogation cages projected on the wall; faces, like that of Laird Cregar as police officer Ed Cornell, kept hidden in the dark; eyes illuminated while watching a flickering film of the murdered girl; scenes shot at odd angles; and sweat beading on characters' brows revealed by extreme close-ups.

Some of the stunning cinematography of *I Wake Up Screaming*. (Everett Collection)

Gwen Wakeling's costumes add to the atmosphere. Wakeling moved to Los Angeles when she was young and developed her skills as a designer entirely on her own. Her first job out of high school was making fashion sketches at a department store, but she always wanted to work in the picture business. Her first film job was assisting legendary costume designer Adrian on Cecil B. DeMille's epic *The King of Kings* (1927); a generation later she would win an Oscar® for the director's *Samson and Delilah* (1949).

Wakeling became a costume designer at RKO and after a few years moved on to Fox. In 1933 she became the studio's head of costume design and remained there until 1942. While at Fox she was recognized for making an impact on fashion, and the media often described her as Darryl Zanuck's "fashion creator." In the announcement of a 1936 design award, the press declared: "Hollywood, home of filmland's stars, is increasingly becoming the headquarters for fashions, vieing [sic] with New York and Paris. Gwen Wakeling, young designer, has become one of Hollywood's foremost costume creators. She is the first woman to receive the silver trophy award given semiannually by the Associated Apparel Manufacturers of Los Angeles."

Gwen was one of the few designers who enjoyed creating costumes for men as much as for women. She became a defining voice of Fox, designing wardrobes for its biggest stars—Tyrone Power in ten films and Shirley Temple in fourteen. With *I Wake Up Screaming* she would also be instrumental in establishing the style of the studio's latest stars, Betty Grable and Carole Landis.

Whereas Mary Astor was the perfect femme fatale in *The Maltese Falcon*, Carole Landis was the perfect intrigante in *I Wake Up Screaming*. She brought her real-life experience as an intrigante to the screen. The former Frances Ridste had been acting in Hollywood since 1936, but only six of her parts in thirty-four films had been credited. The Hal Roach fantasy *One Million B.C.* (1940) was her big break, launching the career of her *I Wake Up Screaming* co-star Victor Mature as well.

"The life of glamour ... began with her *One Million B.C.* buckskin costumes in late 1939 and her January 1940 nose job," claimed Landis biographer Eric Gans. Carole became so well known for wearing next to nothing that swimsuit manufacturer Calcraft Knitting Mills hired her to model their designs. A studio publicist dubbed her the "Ping Girl"—a questionable tie to a popular ad that claimed a certain gasoline could change an engine's "ping to purr."

That wasn't enough for Landis. Convinced she could become a big star, she hired a new publicist, whose brainstorm was to create a campaign of protest. Landis rejected her "Ping" title by taking out quarter-page ads in the trade papers, including *Variety*. She went further still, personally sending editors of 100 of the biggest newspapers letters that began: "This is a lament of a fugitive from a leg art career. I want a fair chance to prove myself something more than a curvaceous cutie. I want to get out of bathing suits and into something more substantial."

Her letters went on to ask newspapers not to publish any bathing suit photos sent by the studios.

Above: Gwen Wakeling shows her own flair for fashion in this 1940 photo. (Everett Collection) Below: Carole Landis tries to cover up her famous figure. (GKB Collection)

Many editors, however, chose to include a picture of Landis in a white one-piece swimsuit when they printed her letter of protest. This was likely the goal of the campaign as it only made her 36-25-36 figure more popular. Artist James Montgomery Flagg declared that Carole had "a physical silhouette that is startling, bordering on the magnificent." And *LIFE* magazine gave her an entire spread surrounding the protest. It was the most publicity the actress had ever received, and it continued through the year.

Carole's costumes in *I Wake Up Screaming* showcase that magnificent figure, although Wakeling kept a careful eye on the design to make sure her figure wasn't exposed too much. "Every outfit had to be put past the Production Code to make sure 'her assets' weren't too prominent," said Film Noir Foundation founder Eddie Muller. Still, Wakeling's designs are as sensual as can be and characterize the difference between the sisters. Like Landis, Vicky loves glamour and desperately wants to be a star. "They're going to glamorize me!" she proclaims to Jill. As a "hash slinger" at a lunchroom, Vicky's a nobody. But a makeover causes multiple men to become obsessed with her,

Robin Ray (Alan Mowbray), Larry Evans (Allyn Joslyn), and Frankie Christopher (Victor Mature) wager they can turn a waitress into a star. (Everett Collection)

something that helps achieve her goal of stardom—but ultimately leads to her undoing.

Frankie promises to put Vicky "in a sable wrap and introduce [her] to cafe society," and he does just that one night at the Pegasus Club. She makes her grand entrance in a pale green, bias-cut gown with fluttering cap sleeves; the fabric tucks and folds around her breasts down to a cinched waist. It accentuates everything without revealing anything. It's the kind of goddess gown made famous by fashion designer Madeleine Vionnet that hugged and moved with the body. In the early 1940s it's a style that still reflects the influence of the 1930s—a high round neck accented with a statement choker necklace along with big drop earrings. The ensemble is paired with long white opera gloves that unbutton and reveal her hands.

Vicky gets her sable wrap and a pale green gown that still shows signs of 1930s style—the tucks and folds use extra fabric that would not be permitted during the war. (Everett Collection)

The next morning Vicky steps out of her bedroom in a floor-length, bias-cut negligee. The look is more revealing than her gown from the night before since it is sleeveless, has a deeper décolletage, and the satin fabric hugs more of her body underneath. Wakeling cleverly concealed some of the bodice with an additional overlay of lace and satin ribbons. Also, Landis quickly covers much of the gown with a velvet robe, tying it around her body before she reaches the living room.

On another occasion, Vicky lounges lazily in yet another satin bias-cut nightgown with sheer chiffon shirred over her breasts to keep her cleavage hidden. A sleeveless robe matches the satin and chiffon of the gown.

The audience gets one glimpse of Vicky as a star when the police pull suspects into a room to watch film of her singing "These Are the Things I Love." She wears another daring dress: a sequin gown that's nearly two pieces and exposes much of her midriff. The crop top has details similar to her other costumes with its deep plunging neckline and cap sleeves. An enormous flower brooch is fixed to the center to conceal just enough of her cleavage. A narrow bridge of sequins connects those in her top to the sequins around her hips before flaring into a full skirt. This design hides her belly button, another objectionable part of a woman's body according to the Production Code. The gown has the desired effect: The men watching her sing can barely contain their lust for her. Everything in Vicky's wardrobe is meant to be both glamorous and seductive.

To contrast the bad-girl attitude of Carole Landis, Betty Grable was cast as Vicky's good-girl sister. After being known for musicals, Grable took a different path with the serious subject matter of *I Wake Up Screaming*. Elizabeth Grable had worked her butt off in Hollywood since 1929.

Vicky's risqué satin and chiffon lounging gown flaunts the famous Landis figure. (Greenbriar Collection)

A veteran of glamorous musicals, Grable navigates a much darker world in *I Wake Up Screaming*. (Everett Collection)

At age twelve she conned her way into the movies by convincing casting agents and producers she was fifteen. She started with Samuel Goldwyn as one of his original "Goldwyn Girls" and then signed with RKO where she appeared in musicals like *The Gay Divorcee* (1934), performing numbers like "Let's Knock Knees."

"She was a tough, chorus-girl sort of dame [and] a terrific dancer," actor Robert Arthur said. After a few years she moved to Paramount, where she was cast mostly in college-themed movies, but she did star in a picture with a title that would prove prophetic: *Million Dollar Legs* (1939).

Unfortunately, *Million Dollar Legs* wasn't a hit and the studio decided to drop her. At this point, Grable wanted to drop Hollywood. She "was so sick and tired of it," she proclaimed, but she gave acting one more try, this time on Broadway. There she became a star with the musical *DuBarry Was a Lady* (1940) and caught the attention of Darryl Zanuck.

When Alice Faye fell ill and couldn't appear in Fox's *Down Argentine Way* (1940), Zanuck signed Betty to a contract, and she began the most successful period of her career. She recalled, "*Down Argentine Way* put me over the top. A superb production, it gave me a once-in-a-lifetime opportunity. Without that chance, I might still be alternating between the stage and screen with indifferent success."

Grable would make three pictures in 1941, including *I Wake Up Screaming*. She was an ideal co-star for Landis, and vice versa. They looked enough alike to be believable as sisters, yet had very different attitudes. Whereas Carole was playing a "sex-loaded" seductress—Zanuck's description of her character—Betty seemed like the girl next door. Vicky is seen slinking around in lingerie, but Jill wears an innocent long-sleeved, floor-length floral nightgown with lace around the lapel of a V neckline. Still, there is a subtle sexiness to Wakeling's design for Jill. Little fabric-covered buttons run all the way down the front of the gown, and they are unbuttoned to her hip so audiences can see a flash of Betty's famous legs when she walks.

Most of Grable's ensembles in the movie continue this look of innocence with high-neck dresses and blouses and a lot of lace accents. Early in the picture, she wears a black dress with a large lace Peter Pan collar. Her last dress is white with lace around the neckline. Jill's costumes alternate between girlish innocence and womanly knowing, especially in the latter part of the film as she wears skirt suits while trying to track down her sister's killer. Although the movie was shot in summer 1941, Grable's outfits are perfectly designed for the fabric-rationed war years to

Grable's tailored suit shows some of the transition from 1930s to 1940s style. (Everett Collection)

Good-girl Jill wears a sweet blouse trimmed in lace, an adornment that would not be available during the war. (Everett Collection)

come—pencil skirts, slim-cut jackets, welt pockets, and lack of lapels.

One of the best is the pin-striped suit Jill wears when she confronts Elisha Cook, Jr., as Harry, the front desk clerk at the sisters' apartment building. The tailoring is exquisite, the fabric cut and carefully aligned so the stripes visually slim her figure while accentuating her assets. It is then accessorized with a brooch and paired with sling-back peep-toe pumps. Grable also wears a checked pencil skirt suit, which is similarly tailored to her figure. It has a streamlined silhouette: a four-button jacket with princess seams and slant welt pockets worn over a blouse with a delicate three-layer rounded collar and petite bow peeking out at the top. All of Betty's looks are accessorized with hair and hats styled vertically (rather than horizontal wide brims, for example) that helped give height to her 5'4" frame.

As a sign that Jill is coming into her own and falling for Frankie, she goes dancing with him at the Pegasus Club in a black ensemble. He first sees her in an all-black coat, which has a V neckline and a tie that cinches in the waist. There are vertical folds in the fabric that act like princess seams in the front and something like a classic sailor collar that hangs down the back. Since black often makes it more difficult to see all the details, a brooch pinned to the breast of the coat adds a little sparkle. The dress underneath is the sexiest that Grable wears in the film. It has the silhouette of lingerie—a slip with spaghetti straps and sheer chiffon over the décolletage to blur away any objections from the Production Code. Additional lace shaped into sleeves makes the outfit seem more innocent.

After the nightclub Jill's look gets more bare when she and Frankie go swimming. It seems a ridiculous turn in a film noir, but this decision came from the very top at Fox. "Fearful that the story line gave Grable and Mature insufficient opportunity for sex appeal," Gans said, "Zanuck added a gratuitous sequence in which the pair go for an evening swim together in order to show off their physiques." Wakeling manages to make the moment seem less odd by designing Betty's black one-piece swimsuit with a silhouette similar to her evening dress. Because of this, the costume seamlessly integrates into Jill's ensemble for the evening as well as her overall wardrobe.

Grable's gams are the perfect accessory for Jill's little black dress. (GKB Collection)

The costumes clearly show the differences between the sisters. (GKB Collection)

I Wake Up Screaming is one of the earliest films noir and deserves to be recognized for establishing some of the style of the genre. It is a great achievement for costume designer Gwen Wakeling in particular because in addition to dressing all the men in the picture, she had to design for two very different actresses and their divergent characters. The film is an opportunity to see Betty Grable and her style in a serious picture two years before she became an icon as the most popular pinup of World War II. The movie is also an opportunity to see the sensual style of Carole Landis in what was ultimately a quasi-autobiographical picture. A real life intrigante and someone who passionately pursued fame in Hollywood, she met a tragic end at age twenty-nine. There's so much about *I Wake Up Screaming* that's worth seeing, especially wardrobes from Wakeling that show the transition into the 1940s and the foundation of film noir style.

Oleg Cassini's costumes in *The Shanghai Gesture* reflect the exoticism of the Art Deco era and sinister attitude of 1940s film noir. (Everett Collection)

The Shanghai Gesture

Premiere: December 26, 1941
Director: Josef von Sternberg
Costume designers: Oleg Cassini; Royer
Studio: United Artists

Not all dark movies fall clearly into the category of film noir. For some, such as *The Maltese Falcon*, there is no debating whether it's noir. The case is less evident for Josef von Sternberg's *The Shanghai Gesture*. Although the film premiered at the end of 1941, its exotic locale makes it feel like a continuation of the romantic fantasy films popular during the Art Deco era, including the director's *Morocco* and *Shanghai Express*.

Noir of the 1940s would more often be set in the dark streets of American cities like San Francisco, Los Angeles, and New York. Although the backdrop of *The Shanghai Gesture* differs, the story fits perfectly within the genre. Set in a casino during the Chinese New Year, the story boasts an unprecedented amount of wickedness, from illicit sex to addiction to murder. As in the best of Sternberg, style is front and center with two different designers creating costumes for the leading ladies.

Gene Tierney's Poppy, the spoiled daughter of rich Sir Guy Charteris (Walter Huston), slinks around in glamorous gowns from Oleg Cassini. Poppy is but a pawn of the casino's owner, Mother Gin Sling, portrayed by American actress Ona Munson. Royer's costumes and Hazel Rodgers' hair and headpieces transform Munson into the Chinese femme fatale. The saying goes that revenge is a dish best served cold and Mother Gin Sling does just that. No one experiences a happy ending in *The Shanghai Gesture* and there's nothing more noir than that.

Style isn't just important to Josef von Sternberg; it's the essence of the man and his movies. Undereducated during his impoverished childhood in Vienna, Sternberg grew up with an incredible visual memory and talent for design. He found inspiration in early films, particularly those of Erich von Stroheim, who infused his work with what Stroheim biographer John Baxter called a "contemplative emotionalism tinged with melancholy." Sets and costumes also played an important part in Stroheim's productions. Sternberg followed this pattern as well and became passionate about lighting, working with great cinematographers such as Lee Garmes to create a signature look that would become influential on the film noir genre.

"He is a poet who writes with images rather than words," wrote Sternberg muse Marlene Dietrich while working on *Morocco*. "And instead of a pencil, he uses light and a camera."

The director would agree. "Without the image, there is nothing," he said. "The eye sees long before the ear hears." Sternberg cared about the script as well. Beginning with *Morocco* in 1930, he found a strong partner in screenwriter Jules Furthman, who would go on in the 1940s to write classic film noir scripts for *To Have and Have Not* and *The Big Sleep*.

To create femme fatale Mother Gin Sling, Royer draped Ona Munson in dramatic, detailed gowns. (GKB Collection)

Furthman's work with Sternberg resulted in some of the director's best pictures, not just *Morocco* but also *Shanghai Express* and *The Shanghai Gesture*. Their collaboration focused on characters, although Sternberg cared less about what his characters said than how they made the audience feel. His poor upbringing prompted him to include the lower class in his pictures and to give villains such glamour it almost washed away any immorality. Perhaps the most famous example of this is Dietrich as the prostitute Shanghai Lily in the proto-noir *Shanghai Express*. Ona Munson would become the "Chinese Dietrich" in *The Shanghai Gesture*.

Best known as Belle Watling in *Gone With the Wind*, Munson was transformed for this film, from the top of her head to the tips of her fingers. The changes began with Hazel Rodgers' wigs and headpieces—true works of art—followed with makeup by Robert Stephanoff. Then Munson was dressed in an extravagant and exotic wardrobe courtesy of costume designer Royer. The dramatic draped, long-

Every kind of sin can be found in Mother Gin Sling's casino, an elaborate set featuring hundreds of extras. (Everett Collection)

sleeved gowns are decorated with maximum detail, including a gold sequin dragon wrapping around Munson in her final costume. In the midst of designing for more than 100 films between 1933 and 1947, Royer along with colleague Gwen Wakeling stepped away from Fox in the early 1940s to start a Beverly Hills boutique. Royer still took occasional freelance assignments, and *The Shanghai Gesture* may have been his most enticing project. Together Royer, Rodgers, and Stephanoff turned the naturally blonde Munson into Sternberg's madam, who makes her grand entrance on-screen after the sound of a gunshot inside the casino.

The Shanghai Gesture was based on John Colton's controversial 1926 play set in a brothel run by Mother Goddam, with Poppy being both promiscuous and an opium addict. The Production Code Administration had rejected more than thirty scripts by producers seeking to bring the story to the screen. Sternberg was determined that this project would be a comeback film for him after his Dietrich collaborations had yielded diminishing returns in the 1930s, so Furthman

Gene Tierney in the film's most influential gown, designed with a sheer, black net bodice and a full, pale pink mousseline de sole skirt. (GKB Collection)

moved the action from a brothel to a casino. The size of that set is staggering, with hundreds of extras wandering around what looks like Dante's circles of hell. Lust, greed, treachery, fraud, wrath, and violence all live within the casino's walls. It's remarkable the administration approved a script dripping that much sin, all of which was forbidden by the Code, from alcohol addiction and prostitution to attempted suicide and murder.

"[It] smells so incredibly evil," Poppy observes on her first visit to the casino. "It has a ghastly familiarity, like a half-remembered dream. Anything could happen here ... any moment." And so, around the Chinese New Year when everyone must pay their debts, Mother Gin Sling exacts vengeance from those who have wronged her. Charteris is her main target by way of his daughter, Poppy.

Gene Tierney plays Poppy perfectly, from her entrance as a conceited, condescending brat to her dramatic decline through addiction. While Tierney found Poppy a challenging character, the actress found enough in Poppy's upbringing she could relate to. Tierney had grown up in a wealthy family, living in New York and Connecticut and attending multiple boarding schools. Like Poppy, she also attended a finishing school in Switzerland. Gene was given the best of everything—her dress as a debutante was a couture copy of Bette Davis' *Jezebel* gown.

Her father, Howard Tierney, was a successful insurance broker with connections to Hollywood and took the family there one summer vacation, visiting several studios and meeting many stars. While the family toured Warner Bros., director Anatole Litvak admired Gene's beautiful face and said, "Young woman, you ought to be in pictures." The comment led to a screen test and an offer of a modest studio contract, but her father didn't think it was the right time or place to begin a career. If the teenager wanted to pursue acting, he would help her do it on Broadway.

Gene's father, like Charteris in *The Shanghai Gesture*, controlled his daughter's life in many ways. He took on the roles of her agent and manager, and his Broadway strategy worked; she was soon discovered on the stage by talent scouts from Hollywood. First came Columbia, which led to an unsatisfying stint at the studio and a quick return to Broadway. She then started acting in a successful 1940 Broadway production of *The Male Animal*, where 20th Century Fox head Darryl F. Zanuck spotted her on stage. In the middle of the play, he told the executive sitting beside him, "Sign that girl." Afterward at the Stork Club, a girl he noticed on the dance floor captivated him. "Forget about that girl in the play," he said. "Sign this one instead. Go find out her name." It was Gene Tierney again and Zanuck was incredulous. "I've tried to sign the same girl twice in a matter of hours and without even realizing it," he said. "Whatever it takes, I want her under contract."

Zanuck's determination led to an arrangement entirely in the actress' favor. Perhaps most significant and contrary to the norm at that time, the terms stated the studio could not force her to change her physical appearance: Her hair could be neither colored nor cut, her slight overbite could not be corrected, and her nose could not be altered with plastic surgery. The contract that protected her like a suit of armor ended up working in everyone's favor for it preserved Tierney's unique beauty.

Another man would soon become the center of Gene's world. Oleg Cassini was an aristocrat, born in Paris to Count Alexander Loiewski and Countess Marguerite Cassini. His mother, a fashion trendsetter throughout Europe, designed dresses for her own shop in Florence. She made regular trips to Paris to study couture collections and took a teenage Oleg along. He showed that he too had a talent for design when his sketches won an international fashion

It's easy to see the allure of Gene Tierney in this gown by Oleg Cassini. (GKB Collection)

competition. His skill as a sketch artist led to an opportunity to work under legendary French couturier Jean Patou. Cassini then opened his own couturier in Italy in 1933 and designed for "the crème de la crème of Roman society." Cassini expressed that he always aspired to capture the glamour he saw in the movies, especially from MGM's head costume designer, Adrian.

In 1936 Cassini bought a first-class ticket to America and arrived in New York with "a tennis racket, a dinner jacket, and a quantity of hope." He also brought a lot of talent and a little luck. Once he moved to Hollywood, he took his racket to the West Side Tennis Club and was paired in a doubles tournament with a manager from Paramount. Not only did they win, but Oleg learned the studio was looking for a designer to help the overworked Edith Head. Cassini quickly secured a position; he worked at Paramount for two years and helped to craft Veronica Lake's style in the feature, *I Wanted Wings* (1941). However, no one would know of his role because he neglected to ask for screen credit in his contract.

Amid the glitz and glamour of Hollywood parties, Oleg Cassini met Gene Tierney. They fell in love but hardly lived a fairy tale. Her controlling family considered Cassini a gold digger, and 20th Century Fox thought he would derail the career of their rising star. The couple eloped to get around the opposition, but in an act of solidarity studios immediately blackballed Cassini.

Gene Tierney and Oleg Cassini on the set. (Everett Collection)

Years later Zanuck would confess to Cassini, "Oleg, it was nothing personal. Gene was a very important property.... We decided to boycott you in the hope that if we made the marriage more difficult, Gene would lose interest in you."

But Gene didn't lose interest, and Oleg continued to design his wife's personal wardrobe even while he was out of work. His efforts caught the attention of Arnold Pressburger, who would soon be producing *The Shanghai Gesture*. When Tierney was loaned to United Artists for the film, the producer quickly hired her husband as the costume designer.

"It's the first really glamorous role I've had. With clothes—and what clothes!" Gene gushed to New York's *Daily News* while in production. Styled by Cassini, she moved from ingenue to sophisticated young woman.

Because *The Shanghai Gesture* had started on-

Above: Mother Gin Sling watches Poppy start to suffer her fate at the roulette table. Below: The slight sloppiness of Poppy's gown reflects the fact that she is out of control and an addict in more ways than one. (Both photos, Everett Collection)

stage, Cassini began there in his research, translating some of the designs from 1926 to 1940s style. But most of the costumes are distinctly his own, featuring all the drama he learned working in European couturiers. They incorporated his own philosophy: "My theory is that all women have curves. These help to make up their charms, and I don't think a dress ought to hide them. It ought to accentuate them. A woman dresses for men. And man isn't interested in the dress; he's interested in the lady inside it. So what I always try to do is to work on a woman, like an architect works on a house—to make her clothes follow her own lines."

Cassini's approach materializes in gown after gown in *The Shanghai Gesture*. The audience first meets Poppy perched at the bar, commenting on the evil atmosphere as if she were above it all. *The Ottawa Journal*, in its review of the picture, paid close attention to wardrobe and noted that Gene wore a relatively simple sleeveless column gown "made of black gossamer chiffon...,

Cassini's costumes flatter the actresses' figures while distinguishing their characters—Dixie (Phyllis Brooks) works at the casino, whereas Poppy exudes wealth. (Everett Collection)

Tierney's sensual sleeveless column gown outlines the contours of her figure. (Everett Collection)

snugly fitted and beautifully draped to outline the contours of her figure." Cassini added drama with a cape that Dr. Omar, played by Victor Mature, uses to suggestively cover and uncover Poppy's bare shoulder. A heavily jeweled necklace from Joseff of Hollywood offers eye-catching detail along with brilliant earrings and a pair of matching bracelets. Adding to the sophisticated feel of this first ensemble, Gene's hair is carefully coiffed in an updo that accentuates her beautiful face.

Another gown Poppy wears shows her at a transition point, no longer able to control her gambling. The dress is arguably the most beautiful she wears in the film and the one that has become the most influential in fashion. As described in *The Ottawa Journal*, the "bouffant dancing dress [combines] a sheer black net bodice and an extremely full pale pink mousseline de sole skirt. [And] splashing across the ... skirt is a trail of appliqued black lace grape clusters." Like Poppy's first gown, this one is accessorized with the same jeweled necklace—a present, she says, from her father. Because her gambling has become an addiction, she pawns the "rope of stones" around her neck at Omar's recommendation to keep going. Little does she realize she has played right into Mother Gin Sling's hands.

Poppy's hair then becomes a sign of her downward spiral into addiction. In the play Poppy succumbs to all the sins the place has to offer, including opium. In the film Omar says, "I wonder what you would look like with your hair down." The suggestion is supremely sexual, but also speaks to her growing loss of control. Soon, she wears her hair down at the roulette table while dressed in what *The Ottawa Journal* writer described as an "intricately draped dinner gown of pale blue Alix jersey ... [with] close-folds at the throat, and deep dolman sleeves [covering] the arms." This dress shows far less structure than the ones before, and it's followed by another with even more draping and a plunging neckline. The silhouettes get looser along with her hair, which is distinctly out of control at this point in the film. Contrast Poppy with Mother Gin Sling, whose hair architecture shows her completely in control at all times.

The final showdown takes place at Gin Sling's grand dinner celebration for the Chinese New Year. It is another remarkable set—a 3,000-square-foot mirror with more than 750 Chinese figures painted on it by artist and actor Keye Luke surrounds the table.

On the sacred holiday when all debts are paid, the guests fail to recognize that they have each wronged their host in some way. Among the fireworks inside and outside the casino, a heavily intoxicated Poppy appears in "a gown that leaves little to the imagination ... made of ivory crepe,

Everyone pays their debts at Gin Sling's dinner celebrating the Chinese New Year. (Everett Collection)

and its snug skirt goes from the floor to ... an inch below the fullness of the hip, whereupon the torso is a glittering mass of gold sequins until it comes to the bustline," noted *The Ottawa Journal*. In this dress, Poppy receives the dragon lady's final punishment.

The Shanghai Gesture, widely considered the last classic Josef von Sternberg film, unspools as a surprising and shocking film noir, from the sordid casino to Poppy's suffering at the hands of femme fatale Mother Gin Sling. As with other Sternberg movies, style tells much of the story as Poppy's gowns become less and less structured, mirroring the woman's disintegration.

Cassini hated the picture and was angry that his "costumes were not even

Poppy's suggestive ivory crepe gown covered in sequins reflects 1930s style. (Everett Collection)

mentioned in passing." In actuality, United Artists released costume photos of Gene in advance of the premiere—including items not in the final picture—and her wardrobe was discussed through the following year. One gown has been an ongoing inspiration in fashion: Descendants of Cassini's dress with the sheer black bodice and full silk skirt appeared in fall 2019 designer collections.

The media loved Oleg Cassini and covered him at length around the release of *The Shanghai Gesture*. A piece written by Frederick C. Othman declared, "The Count has ideas of his own. Unless somebody reaches out and trips him, we predict he's going places in the dress designing business." And he did—Oleg Cassini would become one of the most famous names in fashion after creating Jacqueline Kennedy's classic look. In that regard, even though this film noir's story might not have a happy ending, its style definitely does.

The War Years
1942–1945

The Sky's the Limit!

KEEP BUYING WAR BONDS

Women flooded the workforce during the war years.
(GKB Collection)

Patriotic Style

From December 1941 to September 1945, America was at war.

The military mobilized at once with millions enlisting and millions more drafted, and by the end of the war, more than 12.2 million men and women had served in the armed forces. In addition, much of the country's strength came from those not in uniform. "America's greatest weapon was its industrial might," declared historian Michael Uschan. "The nation's productive capacity was larger than that of all Axis countries combined." The United States possessed natural resources that others did not along with a passionate and seemingly inexhaustible workforce. At the peak of the Great Depression in 1933, unemployment stood at 24.9 percent with 13 million people out of work. By 1943, in the midst of the war, unemployment had dropped to 1.9 percent with jobs available to almost anyone who wanted to work.

At first, companies tried to fill positions with men only, but it soon became clear that women were needed. The attitude shifted from grudging acceptance to all-out publicity campaigns from the Office of War Information that played on women's patriotism to get them working. Women would make up 36 percent of the workforce—peaking in 1944 with more than 19 million women in war-related jobs. Thanks to concepts like Rosie the Riveter, women were accepted as capable of any type of job. They worked everywhere from factories, railroads, and mines to newspapers and radio stations. Their adaptability benefited the war effort, but their presence in the workforce continued to threaten some men. This mood was reflected in the women of film noir where, as historian Molly Haskell says in *From Reluctance to Rape*, "relationships are rooted in fear and suspicion, impotence and inadequacy."

Every resource was prioritized to the war effort, creating shortages and rationing of a great

STOCKINGS

PAINT WHAT
THEY USED
TO BE

One substitute for those used-
be-shimmering silky stockings
plain paint. One simply puts
one's hose with a paint brush a
takes off one's hose with soap a
water. One wonders when and
there is ever a real clothing sho
age whether one will dress co
pletely in a coat of paint—seve
coats in cold weather, we s
pose. These are strange tim

She knows where to draw the line. Right down
the center of the calf. Things are not always what
they seam, when it's a seam you are painting.

Above left: A woman reads over the rationing guidelines in 1942. (Everett Collection) Above right: Women work around the short-age of silk stockings. (GKB Collection)

number of consumer products. This list included fabrics such as leather, wool, and silk that were needed by the military. Silk, in particular, was in short supply because much of it had been imported from overseas—mostly from Europe and Japan—and that would not be possible again until after the war. The U.S. government established the War Production Board (WPB) to direct procurement of materials, and this agency would become the impetus for 1940s style.

In March 1942 the WPB and its subsidiary, the Civilian Production Administration (CPA), released a series of rules for the apparel industry. Limitation Order 85 controlled the amount of material used in women's clothing, and the list of restrictions dictated the austere designs of the decade. L-85's limitations on the length and circumference of skirts made hemlines higher and silhouettes more streamlined. It set maximum measurements for the widths of waistbands, hems, and cuffs. Every adornment and detail of a design—pockets, pleating, tucking, shirring, or quilting—were controlled. Even colors were limited to conserve chemicals for wartime use. Double-breasted coats and jackets were phased out, affecting men's fashions. Further, the WPB eliminated vests, patch pockets, cuffs, and the extra pair of trousers that typically accompanied a man's suit, resulting in fifty million pounds of wool diverted to other uses each year of the war.

Because new clothes were rationed, "make do and mend" became a popular motto on the home front. Home-sewn clothes, which originally were not subject to the garment industry's regulations grew in popularity. Fashion historian Kristina Harris notes, "Paper patterns and sewing supplies were at an all-time high."

Booklets, pamphlets, and magazines shared how to repurpose household items such as tablecloths and curtains for clothing à la *Gone With the Wind*. Patterns appeared for cutting up men's suits to create ones for women. Licensed sewing patterns featured fashions from the studios' most stylish stars, including Olivia de Havilland, Margaret Sullavan, and Betty Grable, named the "Forces' Favorite" pinup.

The shortage of silk stockings posed a problem at a time long before women went barelegged under dresses and skirts. Cosmetic companies started offering something of a solution: Elizabeth Arden, Max Factor, and L'Oréal sold bronze leg lotion that helped to simulate the look

Veronica Lake demonstrates the danger of long hair for factory workers who emulate her style. (GKB Collection)

of stockings. Because real stockings had seams, women went so far as to draw lines up the backs of their legs with eyebrow pencil.

Being fashionable had become more challenging, yet looking good was promoted as part of a woman's patriotic duty. Hollywood was there to help lead the way. Costume designers had always been trendsetters, but they really became beacons of style once Paris fell to Hitler in 1940 and couturiers lost their customers abroad. The designers relished this role since many—including Irene, Jean Louis, Bonnie Cashin, and Oleg Cassini—had made their start in the fashion industry, and they became skilled at predicting trends to make sure their designs remained current. Extensive overlap developed between film and fashion during the war, especially because these costume designers also had boutiques or lines of their own. This was also true of Vera West, Edward Stevenson, Helen Rose, Gwen Wakeling, and Royer.

The influence of costume designers was enormous during the war because everyone went to the movies. "Theatres ran continuously around the clock to accommodate hordes of defense workers, who for the first time in years had money to spend and nothing to spend it on. About the only thing that wasn't rationed was the movies," said Ronald Haver in *David O. Selznick's Hollywood*. According to the Motion Picture Producers and Distributors of America, weekly attendance in picture palaces grew from 85 million people in 1941 to around 95 million by 1945. This means Hollywood was inspiring 68 percent of the U.S. population.

Communication was of the utmost importance during the war, so President Roosevelt appointed a liaison between the government and Hollywood, declaring, "The American motion picture is one of the most effective mediums in informing and entertaining our citizens."

Motion pictures also proved an invaluable tool for building morale, as when costume designers helped shape the attitude toward wartime rationing. As early as February 1942, a month before L-85 took effect, Paramount's lead costume designer Edith Head pronounced:

Oleg Cassini with wife Gene Tierney—wearing her celebrated gown from *The Shanghai Gesture*—and Rita Hayworth. (GKB Collection)

"This year a woman has a new duty, as her wardrobe must reflect the spirit of sacrifice through its adaptability. It must reflect the spirit of enthusiasm through its brightness. It must reflect the spirit of determination through its lack of ostentation. This sacrifice, enthusiasm, and determination will make the woman behind the man in the defense lines a willing and inspirational factor in winning the war."

Head was a master publicist who worked extensively with the media, sitting for interviews and appearing as an expert on radio programs related to style. What she said mattered. To combat the deprivation many women were starting to feel due to war rationing, she announced, "All designers are turning to cotton. Silk is out of style for 1942." Of course, silk was unavailable to civilians, but Head made it seem unfashionable to want to wear silk. It was the birth of patriotic style.

Because rationing made it harder to dress like the stars, hair and makeup took on more importance. In that regard the biggest trendsetter during the war years was Veronica Lake. The 1930s had been dominated by short hairstyles, and Lake's long, blonde "peek-a-boo" look was a revelation. *LIFE* magazine dedicated three pages to her hair in November 1941—broken

This resource helped women make the most of what they already had at home. (Everett Collection)

into "Facts and Figures," "Care and Training," and "Perils and Problems." Her hair would reach iconic status the following year with the films noir *This Gun for Hire* and *The Glass Key*. The perils and problems Veronica experienced became common to an entire nation of emulators and ultimately required government intervention in 1943, resulting in a public service campaign. Veronica would soon be seen wearing victory rolls as well as snoods and turbans.

World War II gave birth to patriotic style, and film noir was the perfect incarnation of the austere and streamlined look of the 1940s. Although costume designers would continue to have nearly unlimited resources, they were careful to create aspirational looks combined with styles that reflected the restrictions women faced during the war. Hollywood proved women could face every challenge without sacrificing style.

Veronica Lake smolders in the gown from *This Gun for Hire* that established her signature style. (Everett Collection)

This Gun for Hire

Premiere: May 13, 1942
Director: Frank Tuttle
Costume designer: Edith Head
Studio: Paramount

Before Bogart and Bacall, there was Ladd and Lake.

Alan Ladd and Veronica Lake appeared together in three films noir in the 1940s. Collectively, these films are influential for their style and for the credibility of the source material—*This Gun for Hire* was based on the Graham Greene novel, *The Glass Key* on the Dashiell Hammett novel, and *The Blue Dahlia* was Raymond Chandler's only produced original screenplay. These movies may owe their origins to giants of crime fiction, but they still needed to be translated to the screen. The person largely responsible for bringing their style to life was Edith Head.

With a six-decade career, eight Oscars, and thirty-five Oscar nominations—no other costume designer comes close to these numbers—Head might well be Hollywood's best-known designer. Her accomplishments grow in significance considering she had no training in fashion, unlike her contemporaries. Instead, Edith Head's background included a master's degree in Romance languages from Stanford and teaching experience at the Hollywood School for Girls. Aside from taking night classes at the Chouinard Art Institute (now the California Institute of the Arts), Edith possessed no real experience in design. This is why in 1924 when Paramount's head costume designer Howard Greer advertised for an assistant, Head felt the need to bluff her way through the interview by claiming sketches borrowed from her classmates as her own. Greer recalled, "There were architectural drawings, plans for interior decoration, magazine illustrations, and fashion designs. Struck dumb with admiration for anyone possessed of such diverse talents, I hired the gal on the spot."

Greer soon saw that Head was ill-equipped to handle the job and forced her to confess her

Edith Head was instrumental in establishing the style of film noir. (Everett Collection)

deception. However, the young woman's audacity impressed him, and he kept her on as his assistant. Greer and colleague Travis Banton began to teach Edith the business, from design to production. Not only was Edith a quick study, but she proved a strong manager and gifted politician, two valuable assets for artists working in the studio system. It became obvious to Greer and Banton that they had hired a talented designer after all.

By 1938 both men had departed Paramount, and Edith found herself leading the studio's costume design department. During her tenure, she would be responsible for iconic costume designs—from Dorothy Lamour's trademark sarong to the strong look of the Hitchcock Heroine. Head was instrumental in establishing the style of film noir. With her love of clean lines and smart tailoring, she perfectly suited the genre.

Edith Head's first film noir coincided with the first teaming of Lake and Ladd. Lake began work at Paramount in 1939 and quickly became a star. Originally billed under her real name, Connie Keane, she was reborn as Veronica Lake in 1941's *I Wanted Wings*. The same year she co-starred with Joel McCrea in *Sullivan's Travels*, which proved popular with the public as well as the critics. This success would give her top billing the following year in *This Gun for Hire*. As with *Flying Down to Rio* (1933) co-stars Fred Astaire and Ginger Rogers, *This Gun for Hire* didn't start out as a plan to pair the actors. In fact, Lake's love interest in the film is Robert Preston. Ladd plays contract killer Philip Raven who works with Lake's character, nightclub entertainer Ellen Graham, to take down a wartime traitor. Ladd's status as an unknown is reflected in the opening credits of *This Gun for Hire*, which conclude with "introducing Alan Ladd."

Ladd and Lake enjoyed natural chemistry and their shared screen time displays similar acting styles and dry delivery. They were complementary in another important way—their height. He stood about 5'6" and Veronica a tiny 4'11". Head, who was just 5'1" and worked with other petite stars such as Gloria Swanson, remembered of Lake, "Her figure problems seemed insurmountable. She was … possibly the smallest normal adult I had ever seen."

Lake's lack of height had to be addressed in the design. Fortunately, Edith found a certain asset to work with. "[Veronica] had big breasts," she said, "which made her seem like a larger woman [on-screen]." However, the Production Code included restrictions about cleavage, so designs had to highlight Veronica's décolletage without revealing too much.

Her wardrobe also was extremely fitted to make her seem taller, with most designs including what one reporter described as a "bodice that [molded] Veronica's torso as if it were sculptured." Floor-length gowns were common in her wardrobes because they elongated her and allowed platform pumps to be hidden underneath. In addition, costumes generally were kept to a single color, and design details "had some type of vertical interest," Edith said.

Lake's entrance in *This Gun for Hire*—wearing a gold lamé gown to perform the musical number "Now You See It"—illustrates Edith's approach. Important elements of the design include the floor length, a long, fitted torso, and long sleeves. The design also features an open V neckline, which further elongated Lake, and Head added ruching to enhance her star's breasts. It would become Veronica's signature style, seen in gowns in subsequent films like *The Glass Key* and *The Blue Dahlia*. These design details also appear in her day dresses, such as the keyhole

Head chose every detail of this gown to give Lake the illusion of height. The full length also hides her massive platform heels. (GKB Collection)

rust-colored crepe dress in *This Gun for Hire*. That garment also included small shiny gold motifs sewn in near the shoulders to help draw the audience's eye upward.

Other costume choices from the color to the accessories in *This Gun for Hire* helped accomplish the task of making the star seem taller. Head often made Lake's outfits monochromatic to give the illusion of height on-screen. Her royal blue suit from *This Gun for Hire* is a good example. The single color, broad shoulders, and nipped waist of its jacket, four-button design, and slim, slightly flared skirt all work to elongate her. Another example is the all-black fishing ensemble she wears while singing "I've Got You." The outfit seems risqué yet it carefully honors the restrictive Production Code. Its sex appeal stems from her vinyl, thigh-high black boots and matching hat. Veronica's hats, especially those that significantly differed from styles worn by other actresses, also added height. Broad-brimmed hats were all the rage at the time, as donned by Bette Davis in *Now, Voyager* (1942) and Ingrid Bergman in *Casablanca*. In contrast, milliners at Paramount made each of Lake's hats with vertical rather than horizontal detail.

Lake wasn't the only *This Gun for Hire* player who benefited from Head's costume design magic. Unlike many of her contemporaries, Edith relished the opportunity to design for men. Ladd is legendary for his impact on men's style, and Edith's design decisions helped give both height and size to his frame. In *This Gun for Hire*, he wore a trench coat through most of the movie. His coat was just a bit longer than it should have been which, like Lake's floor-length

Lake's royal blue suit includes a hat with vertical rather than horizontal detail to give her more height. (Everett Collection)

gowns, helped to elongate him. In *The Glass Key*, he started to be outfitted in the suits that would become his look, with special attention paid to slightly exaggerated tailoring—broader shoulders, longer double-breasted jackets, and sleeves that stretch to cover the cuffs of his white shirts. Ladd's shirt collars also rise a bit higher than usual above his jackets. None of this was noticeable to the average moviegoer.

Great style made Alan Ladd stand out. Turner Classic Movies host Robert Osborne, known for his own impeccable suiting, cited Ladd as his primary inspiration. Fellow TCM host and film noir expert Eddie Muller concurred: "[Ladd] could really wear a suit." Thus, along with *The Maltese Falcon*, Ladd's trifecta of *This Gun for Hire*, *The Glass Key*, and *The Blue Dahlia* proved critical in establishing classic men's style in film noir.

As much as Head's costume designs did for Lake and Ladd, Veronica's hair might have been the biggest hit of all. The cinema of the 1930s had been dominated by short, tight hairstyles. Then came the 1940s and World War II. With clothing in short supply, girls tended to invest in hair and makeup. Lake was a new star with a new look to emulate. Between 1941 and 1943, *LIFE* magazine published five Veronica Lake features and celebrated her hair as a "national treasure."

The trench coat was a staple in film noir and Alan Ladd wore it well. (GKB Collection)

Several stories claim to pinpoint the origin of her trademark style, but Veronica insisted it began during a screen test for *I Wanted Wings*: "[My hair] was very long when I made my test for [Paramount producer Arthur Hornblow, Jr.]. I had a drunk scene and my hair fell over my face. I tried to push it up out of the way, but it kept falling over my face. The executives couldn't agree whether they liked it or not, but decided it would provide something to create talk."

Her seductive, one-eyed gazes at the camera from behind her tresses earned Veronica Lake

Lake's "I've Got You" fishing ensemble seems rather risqué due to vinyl thigh-high boots. (GKB Collection)

the nickname "Peek-a-boo Girl." Her flowing hairstyle would remain popular throughout the decade.

The public was mad for Lake's hair, and Paramount capitalized on its star's popularity. The Ginger Rogers vehicle *The Major and the Minor* (1942) premiered only months after *This Gun for Hire* and includes a scene at a military school dance where the girls all wear the latest styles. "I might as well warn you there's an epidemic at Mrs. Shackleford's school," one of the cadets says to Ginger Rogers. "They all think they're Veronica Lake."

LIFE accommodated when women wanted to know absolutely everything about Lake's hair—its length (seventeen inches in front and twenty-four in back), whether it was bleached (it wasn't), and of course her daily ritual ("shampooed twice, treated with oil, and rinsed in vinegar each morning," Veronica reported). When even this amount of detail wasn't enough, sensational stories arose, such as how Lake supposedly rubbed melted butter into her scalp every few nights. Of course, the studio pounced on the merchandising opportunity. Every woman could feel glamorous with a Veronica Lake hairbrush from the Fuller Brush Company. The frenzy over her hair even became part of the war effort—Lake auctioned off a lock of her hair for $180,000 in war bonds in 1942. She had become one of the hottest pinup girls for men fighting overseas and a style inspiration for women on the home front.

Women's determination to copy Lake's hairstyle presented one problem: During the war, many women worked in defense plants and factories where it proved impractical, even danger-ous, to wear long hair that dropped over one eye and could get caught in machinery. As more women duplicated the style, it became a safety issue. As a result, the government approached Lake in 1943 to change her look. And change she did. Lake began denouncing the peek-a-boo and advertising a new style: She took part in a "Safety Styles" wartime short film to show how to create "victory rolls" to tidy up the look. She then posed again for *LIFE*, but this time in a new style claiming, "Any woman who wears her hair over one eye is silly."

It didn't take long to see changes in her hair. Even as early as *The Glass Key*, her locks were tamed in various ways—rolled into buns at the nape of her neck for one scene and tucked into snoods for others. By *The Blue Dahlia*, Lake's hair is noticeably shorter, although this was due primarily to changing trends. Those trends prompted Lake to cut her hair toward the end of the decade; many say cutting her hair also cut short her career.

But in 1942, Lake dominated. *This Gun for Hire* became a hit with audiences, and she enjoyed status as Paramount's biggest star. Her look, her attitude, and her roles—especially in film noir—prevailed for much of the decade. Newspaper columnist Mayme Ober Peak wrote in

Lake's keyhole, rust-colored crepe dress incorporates many design details to elongate her figure, such as its long sleeves, open neckline, and sculpted waist. (Both photos, GKB Collection)

Even in *This Gun for Hire* Lake's famously long hair was tamed by hats. (Everett Collection)

April 1942 that Veronica was the "most publicized figure since Clara Bow." Lake's costumes were featured in movie magazines like *Modern Screen* and *Photoplay*.

Ironically, her sultry screen persona was in direct contrast to her real one. Introverted and shy and battling mental illness, she felt distinctly different from her characters and image. Like Rita Hayworth, Lake found it impossible to live up to expectations. She felt such a disconnect that during her frequent fittings in sexy gowns, she used to tell Edith, "Pardon me while I put on my other head."

Of course, it's her head she's best known for. Plenty of people have never seen a Veronica Lake film but know her name because of her signature hairstyle. Women channel her look on just about every red carpet. But with Edith Head's help, Lake's contributions to style go far beyond her hair. The suit, keyhole dress, and floor-length gown from *This Gun for Hire* were all popular—stores sold patterns for the outfits so women could make their own—and the designs continue to be influential in fashion. Films such as *L.A. Confidential* (1997) and *The Curse of the Jade Scorpion* (2001) feature similar costume designs. It's fitting that Veronica Lake played a magician in *This Gun for Hire* because she cast a spell over the country in 1942 that can still be felt today.

Opposite: Veronica Lake and Alan Ladd are one of the great screen couples, and their film noir style continues to inspire. (Everett Collection)

Barbara Stanwyck plays the ultimate femme fatale Phyllis Dietrichson in *Double Indemnity*. (Everett Collection)

Double Indemnity

Premiere: September 7, 1944
Director: Billy Wilder
Costume designer: Edith Head
Studio: Paramount

From the moment it begins with Miklos Rozsa's haunting score and what film critic Robert Horton called its "doom-laden thump of a funeral march," *Double Indemnity* draws you into its world of greed, lust, and betrayal. Merely mentioning the title conjures up all the conventions of noir—the voice-over narration, shadowy cinematography, and of course, a manipulative femme fatale—all of it set against the backdrop of 1940s Los Angeles. *The Maltese Falcon* may be considered the first film noir, but *Double Indemnity* is widely considered the best.

The origin of the picture lies in a true story. Two years before the 1929 stock market crash, New York housewife Ruth Snyder murdered her husband to collect on his life insurance policy. In fact, she confessed to tricking him into signing a personal injury policy that paid double in case of death. In the sensational trial that followed, Ruth's lover Judd Grey described her as a "Tiger Woman" in bed as a way to explain his part in the crime. Author James M. Cain along with the rest of America became fascinated by the case, and its eroticism inspired his novels *The Postman Always Rings Twice* and *Double Indemnity*, published in 1934 and 1935, respectively. His next book, *Mildred Pierce*, would see release six years later, and all three became the basis for iconic films noir of the 1940s. Biographer and critic Robert Polito said that "sex would supply the current and currency" of Cain's crime fiction. His gift was creating nuanced women who murder while empathizing somewhat with their motivations to do so.

Director Billy Wilder teamed with Raymond Chandler, author of other popular novels on which films of the genre were based, to adapt *Double Indemnity* as a screenplay. The often-contentious collaboration of Wilder and Chandler created *Double Indemnity*'s tension and sharp banter. Lines from the film continue to be quoted with affection, such as, "How could I have

Double Indemnity challenged the Production Code in many ways, including introducing the character Phyllis Dietrichson wrapped only in a towel. (GKB Collection)

known that murder can sometimes smell like honeysuckle?"

Murder as the centerpiece of the movie enhanced the challenge for Wilder. The Production Code dictated that "filmmakers were forbidden to depict details of a crime that might permit its imitation in real life." In the case of *Double Indemnity*, censorship boss Joseph Breen stated that the script was a "blueprint for murder." Eight years of changes followed before the screenplay could get approval. And when it did, it was "the first time a Hollywood film explicitly explored the means, motives, and opportunity of committing a murder," according to film noir authority Eddie Muller.

The talented Billy Wilder had recently made the jump from screenwriter to director; *Double Indemnity* was his third chance at the helm after *The Major and the Minor* and *Five Graves to Cairo* (1943). His first try at film noir is renowned for the dialogue and also celebrated for its visual style thanks to Wilder's partnership with cinematographer John Seitz, who had already made a mark in film noir with *This Gun for Hire* and would work with Wilder on both *Double Indemnity* and *Sunset Boulevard*. Seitz picked up where Josef von Sternberg left off in proto-noir *Shanghai Express*, using shadows, including those of venetian blinds, to dramatic effect. Throughout *Double Indemnity* blinds cast symbolic shadows across the faces of the murderers. Seitz created mood in every scene and found ingenious ways to do so. For instance, since dust is imperceptible to the camera, he and Wilder blew aluminum particles into the air to make the living room of the Dietrichsons—the family at the center of the story—look dark and dirty.

Dark and dirty also aptly describes femme fatale Phyllis Dietrichson. Wilder wanted only one woman to play the part: Barbara Stanwyck. Although she expressed being "a little afraid after ... years of playing heroines to go into an out-and-out killer," Stanwyck accepted the challenge. She already had an admirer in Billy Wilder, who respected the authenticity of her performances.

"Stanwyck brought an edge of reality to every role she played," John Kobal wrote after interviewing her. "Even if it wasn't natural to her, she made it look natural." This talent is apparent in her portrayal of the murderess Phyllis, who had clearly struggled in life. Stanwyck had more than enough struggles of her own to be able to empathize with the character. Born Ruby Stevens, she was orphaned at age four when her mother died as a result of a streetcar accident and her father heightened that tragedy by abandoning his family. As a result, Stanwyck spent her childhood drifting between foster care and the homes of family members. Inspired by her older sister Mildred's life as a showgirl, Stanwyck danced her way into the Ziegfeld Follies lineup at fifteen. This led to dramatic acting roles on Broadway and ultimately a trip to Hollywood.

Columbia Pictures' *Ladies of Leisure* (1930) put Barbara Stanwyck on the path to screen stardom. It was the first of five films directed by her mentor, Frank Capra, who tapped into Stanwyck's natural talent and experience. Her characters seemed to share a common condition: "Whatever comforts they were offered, won or inherited, they never forgot the hard times," Kobal described. This theme continued in Barbara's career when she moved to Warner Bros., the studio where she would star in *Baby Face* (1933). The character of Lily in that pre-Code classic, with her relentless pursuit of money, was a perfect precursor to Phyllis in *Double Indemnity*. Barbara

The character Lily in the pre-Code *Baby Face* (above) was a precursor to Phyllis in *Double Indemnity*. (Above, GKB Collection; below, Everett Collection)

Edith Head was gifted at designing women's suits. This one worked for both the character and the actress, who had a no-non-sense style. (Everett Collection)

worked at nearly every studio through the end of the 1930s, from contracts with Columbia and RKO to freelance arrangements with others. She was consistently seen as a great actress by studio executives wherever she worked—but not a great beauty. That would all change when Stanwyck began working at Paramount and met head costume designer Edith Head.

Head understood the needs of both actress and character and found herself assigned frequently to the talented Stanwyck, who was known for not being terribly interested in glamour. To Stanwyck, being natural was of the highest importance. She was also known inside the studios for having some challenges with her figure. Her biographer Victoria Wilson summed up the issues: "Barbara was 5'3", with broad shoulders and back, a long waist, and flat buttocks that then extended outward."

That long waist was perhaps the biggest design challenge Edith was forced to address. Head explained that she gave the appearance of lifting Stanwyck's waistline "by widening the waistbands on the front of her gowns and narrowing them slightly in back."

Paramount's *The Lady Eve* (1941) would be a career-changing project for both women. The studio's lead costume designer had already made an impact with the sarong for Dorothy Lamour in several pictures set in the South Seas, but *The Lady Eve* was Edith Head's first real foray into fashion in film. The exquisite wardrobe she created for Stanwyck included a two-piece, midriff baring, short-sleeved beaded gown. Barbara felt truly glamorous for the first time and suddenly found herself setting trends in fashion. The wardrobe gave her a new perspective and a new appreciation for clothes. Stanwyck said, "Nobody understands my figure as well as Edith Head."

The inspiration for Stanwyck's wardrobe in *Double Indemnity* came from multiple sources—the novel, the screenplay, and Head. Stanwyck's earliest scenes make it clear Phyllis is superficial and wants to be seen as a wealthy woman. Some of this is accomplished by adorning Stanwyck in stunning Joseff of Hollywood jewelry, in particular a gold anklet with Phyllis' name engraved on it. Cain makes no mention of an anklet in his novel; the screenplay of Wilder and Chan-

Double Indemnity's famous anklet does not appear in James M. Cain's novel. It first appeared in the screenplay and was brought to prominence by costume designer Edith Head. (Everett Collection)

Plotting a murder in style: Phyllis wears a black pencil skirt, a white bishop-sleeved blouse, and a wool houndstooth vest. (Above, GKB Collection; below, Everett Collection)

Even around the house, Phyllis wears glamorous dresses and an enormous ring to flaunt her wealth. (Everett Collection)

dler includes the anklet in what has become a legendary entrance in noir: "Phyllis Dietrichson stands looking down. She is in her early thirties. She holds a large bath towel around her very appetizing torso, down to about two inches above her knees. She wears no stockings, no nothing. On her feet a pair of high-heeled bedroom slippers with pom-poms. On her left ankle a gold anklet."

The anklet proves so important that it's even woven into the dialogue in a seductive exchange between Phyllis and her lover Walter Neff (Fred MacMurray). In fact, it's how he learns her name.

The anklet is far from her only piece of ornamentation. Phyllis also shows off an enormous ring, seen on her wedding ring finger but looking large enough to be a cocktail ring. Wilder features the ring in many shots, especially when Phyllis is on the phone, and it's frequently paired with a large link bracelet.

Phyllis' clothes give the character other opportunities to flaunt her status. Even at home, she wears the most glamorous of dresses. She changes from her towel into a belted, long-sleeved pale blue summer dress with ruffles around the buttons and sleeve cuffs. For Neff's next visit, Wilder directed the costume to be "a gay print dress with a wide sash over her hips." Head reinterpreted this as a long-sleeved, floor-length gown with a floral print bodice and solid skirt. This dress in particular, with its dropped waist in the back, shows off Edith's technique for correcting Stanwyck's long torso. There is also some of Veronica Lake's signature style in this costume, from the floor length and long sleeves to the V neckline and ruching around the bust that also helped to balance Barbara's proportions. Many of those design elements are incorporated into the final costume of the film as well: the white silk jumpsuit she wears while waiting for Walter, an ensemble that would inspire fashion designers like Halston in the 1970s.

Some of the costumes in the film were entirely Head's decision. When Phyllis first visits Walter at his apartment, she wears a pale cardigan sweater worn backward—a style popular in the 1940s—black trousers, and belted camel's hair coat. It seems a strategic move on Phyllis' part, downshifting into a more innocent ensemble to try to reel Walter back in. The sweater is subtle but still overtly sexy, revealing her bra beneath it. The cardigan caused such a commotion that even during filming in 1943, Hollywood gossip columnist Sidney Skolsky said to Stanwyck, "But the sweater. The sweater! How did the Hays Office ever let that get by?"

Another costume attributed solely to Edith is the one Phyllis wears to the grocery store. The screenplay asked for a "simple house dress [and] no hat." Instead, Head decked her out in a black pencil skirt, white bishop-sleeved blouse (a favorite style of Stanwyck), and a wool houndstooth vest. Edith also conceived of the short-sleeved fringed dress in black, a significant color choice considering Phyllis wears it when she tricks her husband into buying accident insurance.

Wilder made one controversial style contribution to *Double Indemnity*. In the novel Cain describes Phyllis as having "dusty blonde hair," but the director took it further with an over-the-top bleach-blonde wig. Stanwyck didn't find the wig to be an issue; she was accustomed to wearing them. In *Baby Face* she had worn not one but seven wigs that reflected the character's evolving glamour as she climbed the social and financial ladder. The *Double Indemnity* wig was different: Wilder used it to make Phyllis "look as sleazy as possible." Although the intention was understood, the style was hated from the start. Wilder biographer Kevin Lally quoted Par-

Phyllis, appropriately wearing a fringed dress in black, watches her husband seal his fate. (Everett Collection)

Nothing from *Double Indemnity* continues to cause more controversy than Stanwyck's bleach-blonde wig. (Greenbriar Collection)

amount production head Buddy De Sylva: "We hired Barbara Stanwyck, and here we get George Washington." The wig has continued to be criticized for seeming too fake, but Wilder insisted that was exactly the point. It trumpets "the phoniness of the girl—bad taste, phony wig." Barbara claimed she never knew his reasons for the wig and simply carried out her director's vision for the character; she later confessed to Hedda Hopper that she even felt sexy in it.

Double Indemnity earned praise for realism at the time of its release and continues to be celebrated for its influential style—from the production design to the costume design. Some costumes merge realism and style, such as the sweater, pants, and camel coat Phyllis wears to Walter's apartment. Her trousers, in particular, are in lockstep with what women were wearing during the war years, especially since so many found themselves working in factories.

Double Indemnity continues to be a reference for fashion designers; the black short-sleeved fringe dress and white silk jumpsuit remain on trend. The wardrobe has also influenced other costume design, the most obvious example being Carl Reiner's comedy-noir *Dead Men Don't Wear Plaid* (1981). Reiner hired Edith Head to design the costumes, and she paid tribute to many films noir, including her own work from *Double Indemnity*. Fittingly, Reiner's movie would be Head's swan song; she passed away five months after the premiere. That same year, Lawrence Kasdan's neo-noir *Body Heat* (1981) also paid tribute by taking its plot and costume cues right from *Double Indemnity*. Whether influencing other films or inspiring fashion, *Double Indemnity* is all about style, straight down the line.

Costume designer Bonnie Cashin begins Laura's makeover with this fashion-forward floral gown. (Alamy Collection)

Laura

Premiere: October 11, 1944
Director: Otto Preminger
Costume designer: Bonnie Cashin
Studio: 20th Century Fox

Laura opens as if a romance, with David Raskin's lush musical score playing as the credits appear over a portrait of a beautiful woman. Suddenly, the screen goes black and a man's voice begins, "I shall never forget the weekend Laura died."

With one line, the audience is drawn into the mystery of this film noir. Ethereal Gene Tierney plays the intrigante Laura Hunt, a young career woman who first appears to be the victim of murder and then eventually becomes the main suspect. Producer and director Otto Preminger so loved the twists and turns in Vera Caspary's 1943 book, *Laura*, that he pressed 20th Century Fox head Darryl Zanuck to acquire it for the screen. In those twists and turns, Laura's life is revealed through three men and their obsession with her: newspaper columnist Waldo Lydecker (Clifton Webb), playboy Shelby Carpenter (Vincent Price), and Detective Lt. Mark McPherson (Dana Andrews). The romantic score and high style of the film disguise the darkness within. Laura's circle of New York high society may have a veneer of sophistication, but evil lurks underneath. Style is always important in a movie, especially in film noir, but it's central to *Laura*. Tierney's costumes by Bonnie Cashin communicate the evolution of the character and give new meaning to the concept of fashion in film.

Gene Tierney was perfect for the role of Laura Hunt. She grew up in a wealthy family on the east coast, living in New York and Connecticut, and was educated in boarding schools as well as a finishing school in Switzerland. She circulated among the upper crust and exuded the "innate breeding" Lydecker attributed to Laura in the movie. And like Laura, Gene was accustomed to being controlled by men. Her father, Howard Tierney, had directed every aspect of her early life and when her acting career began served as her agent and manager. It was a relationship that

79

would rot. His authority over her finances allowed him to steal everything she made during her first two years in Hollywood, as Gene would disclose in her 1978 memoir, *Self-Portrait*. As if that weren't enough, he then sued her for $50,000 more.

Tierney's father objected to the next important man in her life—young Paramount costume designer Oleg Cassini. Like the men in the movie who fixate on Laura's portrait, Cassini found himself in awe of Gene's beauty. She captivated him when they worked together on *The Shanghai Gesture*. They married not long afterward, but Gene had already felt his influence from the beginning of their relationship when he controlled what she wore. Tierney had always been passionate about fashion and thoughtful about her ensembles, even designing many herself. Yet she recalled of their first date: "Oleg strode in the door, took one look at [my outfit] and almost passed out. 'I won't take you out dressed like that!' he bellowed. 'First, take off the hat and cape and then go get a navy bag. Forget the gloves, if you don't have any navy ones.'"

In his autobiography Cassini would admit to a similar affront when he and Gene were going to a black-tie event. When he arrived at Gene's door, he disliked a dress of her own design. He

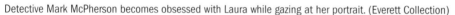

Detective Mark McPherson becomes obsessed with Laura while gazing at her portrait. (Everett Collection)

Waldo Lydecker sets out to improve Laura's style. (Everett Collection)

recalled, "She was not perfect for me…. I said to her, 'Now, we're going to start everything right. The most important thing is not to lie to each other. I don't like your dress. I want you to go change.'"

The episode is suggestive of Waldo Lydecker's attitude and sway toward Laura in the film. An entire sequence in the picture itemizes all he did to "improve" her.

"She deferred to my judgment and taste," Waldo tells McPherson after Laura's alleged death. "I selected a more attractive hair dress for her. I taught her what clothes were more becoming to her."

Lydecker's objectification of Laura creates a sense that Laura's life is not her own. He considers her a possession, an accessory, an extension of his greatness. He says, speaking of himself in the third person, "She became as famous as Waldo Lydecker's walking stick and his white carnation."

As Laura's on-screen style evolves in the film, 20th Century Fox costume designer Bonnie Cashin demonstrates her talent for capturing character in costume and also gives the audience a

The always fashionable Bonnie Cashin during her time designing costumes for Fox. (Courtesy Stephanie Lake, The Bonnie Cashin Archive)

view of her innovations as a fashion designer.

As the world began to move away from couture and to democratize fashion, Cashin helped transform ready-to-wear by making even casual clothes glamorous. She is perhaps best known as one of the founders of the fashion house Coach, but she also designed and produced collections for several other companies, including her own. She won many awards and honors, including induction into the prestigious Coty American Fashion Critics Hall of Fame. The Metropolitan Museum of Art is but one of many institutions that have hosted exhibitions of her work, and her influence lives on through other designers, including Donna Karan and Ralph Lauren. Cashin's origins, however, were in costume design and it remained a passion in her life.

Cashin was born in Oakland, California, and grew up inspired by the San Francisco area, from the unpredictable climate to the exotic mix of cultures. Both had an impact on her designs. She knew how to sew thanks to her mother, a talented dressmaker who opened a shop in every town where the family lived. Eventually, they moved to Los Angeles, and Bonnie became a professional designer while still a teen. Attending Hollywood High School, she made costumes for the live stage acts of producers Fanchon and Marco, whose shows accompanied movie screenings in theaters. Working with those dancers, Cashin developed a talent for "designing clothes that moved well with the body."

In 1934 she moved to the east coast to study at the Art Students League of New York. While attending that school, she became "the youngest designer ever to hit Broadway" when she created costumes for the famed chorus line Roxyettes, as the Rockettes were originally dubbed. It was there at the Roxy Theater that her work was admired by *Harper's Bazaar* editor Carmel Snow and resulted in Cashin's first job in fashion at Adler & Adler.

By 1943 Cashin sought a return to California and costume design. "I felt more at home with dancers, actors, artists, musicians, writers—people like that—than I did with most of the businessmen I'd met in the clothing industry," she said.

Producer William Perlberg became the matchmaker between Bonnie and 20th Century Fox; she eventually designed costumes for approximately sixty of the studio's films. Not long into her contract, Preminger specifically chose her to design what she would consider a dream project: *Laura*. Her team had two months before filming began to work on the costumes. While Cashin claimed "the budget was kept tight," Preminger fought the studio to allow $15,000 for costumes, an amount so extravagant for the time it was reported by the media. He even rented real diamonds and pearls from jewelers rather than use costume jewelry. "His Laura would not be wearing fake jewelry," Tierney's biographer Michelle Vogel declared. Everything was custom-made for her wardrobe, right down to her black lace lingerie trimmed with baby-blue ribbon.

Laura's wardrobe changes with each man in her life. Waldo heightens her glamour to match his own; much of his style stems from New York City and its high society. He first meets Laura when she is an ambitious advertising associate at the Algonquin Hotel. and then starts to dress her for fancy evenings out at Sardi's and El Morocco and for Broadway plays once their relationship is under way. Lydecker's apartment, by his own description, is lavish; he writes his newspaper column in an enormous bathroom with a marble tub, and the rest of his home is filled with priceless possessions. Laura's apartment seems styled by the same hand, and he even claims ownership over several items in it.

In a remarkable makeover montage that captures Waldo's ownership of Laura, Gene dons a dozen costumes that range from a sweeping strapless floral gown to orchid-pink pajamas embellished with sequins. One incredible haute couture moment is her fireside ensemble of a creamy cardigan paired with a belted skirt of gray and white squirrel. This is pure Cashin, as she was among the first in fashion to use leather and furs from leopard to raccoon in basics like dresses and skirts.

Laura's haute couture wardrobe includes a belted skirt of gray and white squirrel. (GKB Collection)

Laura dons the final costume in Lydecker's transformation of her at a black-tie party given by her aunt, Ann Treadwell (Judith Anderson). She wears a white cowl-neck, bias-cut goddess gown accessorized with a brooch over her left shoulder. The breathtaking dress echoes Adrian's designs for Jean Harlow.

"We fitted the clothes on naked bodies," Cashin commented. "It's the movement of a slim body underneath clothes that is sex personified." She added a little extra fabric around the der-riere in the dress to make sure the costume did not provoke objections from the Production Code.

In this gown Laura meets Vincent Price's Shelby Carpenter, and the audience starts to see a subtle shift in her wardrobe. At this point in her journey, she has become successful as an advertising execu-tive. Serving up a rare compliment, Lydecker says, "I gave her her start, but it was her own talent and imag-ination that enabled her to rise to the top of her profession ... and stay there."

Above: Cashin's goddess gown for Laura is reminiscent of Adrian's many bias-cut designs for Jean Harlow. Below: Cashin debuted one of her famous designs—the "Spaniel's Ears" hat—in *Laura*. (Both photos, Everett Collection)

Laura's position allows her to give Shelby the job he says he craves. However, his ambition seems solely to get close to her and her money rather than to pursue a career. Lau-ra's work wardrobe includes a skirt suit, a matching knit sweater and skirt set, and a sweater and pencil skirt paired with a collarless jacket with tie closures. This last ensemble is topped with a hat that was the debut of one of Cashin's own styles: the "Spaniel's Ears" hat. Shelby even

compliments her: "I approve of that hat. And the girl in it, too." The style appears again when Laura returns to her apartment after a trip to the mountains. In that hat and a slicker coat soaked from the rain, she finds Dana Andrews as Detective Mark McPherson waiting for her.

When Mark (trench coat and all) moves into the plot with Laura, she adopts a more modern style, even fashion-forward for the early 1940s. It's as if she is finding her own voice, which proves an example of the costume designer's voice as well. Cashin always loved the style of the Far East, and the *Los Angeles Times* reported, "The Japanese kimono was her inspiration for layering and detail such as wide sleeves." Both design features can be seen in the belted, striped wrap top and palazzo pants Laura wears the morning after her return from the "dead."

Bonnie Cashin favored loose-fitting designs that can also be seen in the peasant blouse and matching

Above: The style of Cashin's "Spaniel's Ears" hat is paired with Laura's rain slicker. (GKB Collection) Below: The Japanese kimono inspired many of Cashin's designs, including this belted top. (Greenbriar Collection)

skirt Laura wears at her party. At this point in the picture, she's falling for Mark and positioning herself as a potential wife, even assuring him of her ability to cook—an attempt to separate herself in Mark's mind from the spoiled people who surround her.

"For the first time in ages, I know what I'm doing," she says as she pushes Waldo away while wearing a costume that has hints of a cheongsam dress. The look suggests that Laura is finally coming into her own as a woman.

The public response to Cashin's collection of costumes was immediate and overwhelming.

Laura's style continues to evolve as she asserts her independence. (Everett Collection)

Columnist Marian Christy recounted, "The public relations man blew into her office one day and told Bonnie he had just weighed the press clippings and they added up to ten pounds."

Cashin's spectacular wardrobe for Gene Tierney in *Laura* showcases some of the Cashin signature style as well as communicating so much about the character. "It was exciting work," she said about her time at Fox. "I wasn't designing for fashion, but for characteristics, which is the way I still like to design clothes for daily wear. I like to design clothes for a woman who plays a particular role in life, not simply to design clothes that follow a certain trend."

Among all of its beautiful style is an ominous feeling within *Laura*. It's like a bad dream, as Mark says, with so much stirring beneath the surface. The horror doesn't just concern the murder, but also the discovery that everyone in Laura's life seems capable of that murder.

One reviewer described Laura as the "dazzling glamor girl so many people wanted to kill." Gene Tierney played her like an apparition. She was perhaps at her most beautiful in this film noir, her face luminous under Oscar-winner Joseph LaShelle's lights.

"Laura was a woman of mystery and glamour, unattainable," Gene recalled, "the kind of woman I admired in the pages of *Vogue* as a young girl."

Whether in the portrait or in person, Laura is the result of what men project upon her. Her

costumes reflect the roles she plays in each of her relationships. They also allow the audience to sense some new-found strength at the end of the picture. Cashin astutely understood what was needed in those costumes. She inspired audiences with her signature style expressed in a squirrel-fur skirt, a kimono jacket, and a Spaniel's Ears hat. Her draped goddess gown influenced designs in both fashion and film, including one of Ava Gardner's costumes a decade later in *The Barefoot Contessa* (1954).

In a film where the audience questions what is real and what is fantasy, Cashin includes both in costumes that are clues to the character of Laura as well as fashion inspiration for the war years.

Above: Cashin favored loose-fitting designs and this can be seen in Laura's peasant blouse and matching skirt. (Greenbriar Collection)
Below: Laura's style evolution hints that she's beginning to break away from her social circle. (Everett Collection)

Humphrey Bogart and Lauren Bacall began as a couple, on-screen and off, with *To Have and Have Not*. (GKB Collection)

To Have and Have Not

Premiere: October 11, 1944
Director: Howard Hawks
Costume designer: Milo Anderson
Studio: Warner Bros.

Film noir is known for its darkness and celebrated for it. Darkness saturates stories that center on vices like jealousy and greed and crimes ranging from robbery to murder. It's ironic, then, that a great love story in Hollywood history—some say THE great love story—would be found within the genre of film noir. *To Have and Have Not*, the story of an American boat captain who falls for a beautiful drifter while working with the French Resistance in Martinique, brought Humphrey Bogart and Lauren Bacall together. They would become known for their style, developed in three more noir films: *The Big Sleep* (1946), *Dark Passage* (1947), and *Key Largo* (1948). Audiences watched them fall in love and saw their relationship evolve on-screen, from first contact to successful marriage. It all began with *To Have and Have Not*—specifically, thanks to the wife of its director, Howard Hawks.

According to Bogart and Bacall biographer Joe Hyams, one morning in March 1943, Nancy Gross, aka "Slim" Hawks, reached for her copy of *Harper's Bazaar*. Slim was a socialite and successful model who had graced the magazine's cover through the years and was a perennial selection on its "best dressed" lists. That month's cover featured a sultry eighteen year old with shoulder-length, tawny blonde hair and wide-set green eyes. She wore a dark blue "outfit that made her look like a teen-age Mata Hari," said Hyams. Howard Hawks was then in pre-production for *To Have and Have Not* at Warner Bros. but hadn't been able to figure out whom to cast as the female lead.

"Where the hell am I going to find the right girl?" Hawks grumbled to Slim, who slid the magazine over to him. The girl resembled his wife; both represented the Hawksian "taste in beauty—scrubbed clean, healthy, shining and golden," according to Slim Hawks. "There was definitely a bit of panther about her." And so began the Hollywood career of Betty Perske, then modeling under the name Betty Bacal (with one "l"), who would soon become an actress known all over the world as Lauren Bacall.

Hawks made pictures with strong male leads and also featured strong women, such as Jean Arthur in *Only Angels Have Wings* (1939) and Rosalind Russell in *His Girl Friday* (1940). In *To Have and Have Not* Bogart's self-reliant male would meet up with a wisecracking and aggressive woman in the Hawks tradition. He saw the potential in Bacall and signed the model–stage actress to a personal contract for $250 a week. The director then worked to ensure a successful screen audition for Jack Warner that would bring out her strengths and mold her into the ideal Hawksian woman, which Bogart biographers Sperber and Lax describe as "outspoken, self-assured, sexually aggressive, at once young and ageless."

Bacall on the March 1943 magazine cover that caught the eye of Howard Hawks. (GKB Collection)

Lauren had started performing on the stage in New York but discovered most of her hard work was yet to come in Hollywood. It started with training to lower the pitch of her voice. Bacall would drive to deserted places in Los Angeles—the beach or canyons off Mulholland Drive—and shout lines from books until she grew hoarse. Then she would lean her diaphragm against a board while reading the biblical epic *The Robe* out loud. These vocal exercises, combined with her love of smoking, effectively dropped the register of her voice to the low purr that became her signature.

Blessed with high cheekbones and pouty lips, Bacall began modeling to make ends meet while attempting a career in the theater. Diana Vreeland, famed fashion editor of *Harper's Bazaar*, loved Betty's "affect [and] used her to showcase new dresses and suits." That experience in front of the camera would be invaluable training for her future in Hollywood. But even Bacall's modeling experience, including as a cover girl, failed to do her beauty justice. It took celluloid and Sid Hickox's cinematography in *To Have and Have Not* to really capture her refined feline features—namely her intense almond eyes framed by strong arched brows. *TIME* magazine did a cover story on the actress after her movie debut and effectively summed up her appeal: "What is fascinating about Bacall is not so much her kinetic sea-green eyes or her svelte-as-sin 129-lb. body, but the distillation of glamour into poise, inner amusement, and enriched femininity that no twenty-year-old sex kitten has lived long enough to acquire."

From the start, Bacall seemed different from other actresses of the day, with the worldliness of an old soul who had been there and done that despite her tender age of eighteen. Her New York upbringing lent savvy, and she quickly showed she could be "one of the guys" on the set of *To Have and Have Not*. Street smart yet vulnerable, Lauren would seduce the audience just as she seduced Bogart using that unique, come-hither look. Ironically, although celebrated for a seemingly endless supply of confidence, "The Look" came as the result of trying to keep her nerves in check—lowering her chin to calm her visible shaking. It was a look Hawks would command of Bacall again and again, and it would become immortalized when the young actress delivered the line, "You know how to whistle, don't you, Steve? You just put your lips together and blow."

To Have and Have Not contains so many exchanges of this nature that the *New York Times* commented, "Hers is mainly a job of radiating as much sex as the law will allow." Not surpris-

Bacall's checked suit was inspired by Slim Hawks' personal style. (Everett Collection)

Sidney Hickox's stunning cinematography in *To Have and Have Not* shows why it is a quintessential film noir. (Everett Collection)

ingly, Bogart fell hard for Bacall during filming.

At this point in his career, Bogart was the biggest star at Warner Bros. With the noir *The Maltese Falcon* followed by *Casablanca*, Bogie had successfully made the transition away from the gangster roles that had propelled him through the 1930s. And in the tradition of those two films, *To Have and Have Not* features an outstanding group of artists contributing to the production. In addition to Hawks at the helm, Jules Furthman and William Faulkner developed a screenplay from Ernest Hemingway's novel, and Milo Anderson provided the costume design.

Bogart plays Harry "Steve" Morgan, a boat captain involved with the French Resistance against the Nazi regime during World War II. The plot resembles *Casablanca* and captures some of its magic, especially between Bogart and Bacall. The pair shows chemistry so strong that audiences feel the heat of their growing real-life relationship on-screen. *To Have and Have Not* marks the moment they fall in love—it's captured forever on film.

The inspiration for Bacall's character—the mysterious Marie "Slim" Browning—came from multiple sources. One was Marlene Dietrich; Furthman had scripted several Sternberg–Dietrich films, including *Shanghai Express*, and Hawks asked for the same "surly, sultry Dietrich persona" in *To Have and Have Not*. But Furthman admitted the character had also been based on Slim Hawks. Not only was her nickname incorporated into the film, as was Howard's nickname of

"Steve," but the dialogue included her unique delivery. Many of the movie's most memorable lines came courtesy of Slim's everyday dialogue; she remembered her husband "pencil and pad in hand, jotting down her mots at night, to use them in the morning." Furthman agreed, even believing she deserved script co-credit since so much of the material came from her lips. In the end Bacall reaped the benefits of Slim Hawks' celebrated style.

Bacall could not have been in better hands than those of costume designer Milo Anderson, who had been part of the Warner Bros. costume design trifecta with Orry-Kelly, who had done *The Maltese Falcon* and *Casablanca*, and Leah Rhodes, who had designed gowns for Bogart pictures among others in her work at the studio. Together, they defined the studio's style voice and were instrumental in establishing the style of both Bogart and Bacall.

Anderson embarked on his career at a young age, studying costume design on his own while attending Los Angeles' Fairfax High School and spending summers working at Western Costume. While still a teenager, he was discovered by opera singer Alice Gentle and was asked to design her costumes for the 1923 tour of

Milo Anderson discusses designs with Olivia de Havilland for *Captain Blood* (1935). (Everett Collection)

Carmen. His work was a hit and instilled the young designer with enough confidence to share sketches with costume designer Adrian. A job designing for Samuel Goldwyn's Eddie Cantor vehicle *The Kid from Spain* (1932) followed and then a position at Warner Bros. starting in 1933. Anderson would remain at the studio for nearly twenty years.

Like Orry-Kelly and Rhodes, Milo Anderson was terrifically talented at suiting. The movies of all three designers are known for their suits; many stand out, even during the war years when everyone seemed to be wearing them. For *To Have and Have Not* Anderson styled a tight wardrobe, and the most influential costume is Bacall's gingham suit. Her character wears it when she's introduced, and then dons it again at the end of the

film. Its origins and inspiration lay entirely with Slim. Howard Hawks biographer Todd Mc-Carthy wrote that Slim's "husband used not only her name [but also her] look and clothes." In fact, the suit in *To Have and Have Not* nearly doubles for one from Slim Hawks' own closet. The suit communicates the strong character of the film's *intrigante*, but the gingham pattern, peplum jacket, and snug pencil skirt also convey plenty of sensuality. Origins of the outfit can be seen in Phyllis Brooks' opening costume in *The Shanghai Gesture*—right down to the beret

As a chanteuse, Slim performs in a daring gown of liquid black satin. (GKB Collection)

accessory. The *To Have and Have Not* suit immediately became popular and such a strong example of Hawks–Bacall style that it appeared in another incarnation in their follow-up, *The Big Sleep*.

It wouldn't be Hollywood in the 1940s without a glamorous gown in the picture, and the one Bacall wears to perform the sultry number "How Little We Know" is also memorable with its unique design. Made of liquid black satin, the dress is two pieces connected by an O-ring in front. The top resembles half a jacket—broad-shouldered with long sleeves and a plunging V neckline—and the skirt has the feel of a sarong. Despite the dramatic décolletage and bare midriff, the design manages to avoid censorship by not revealing cleavage or Bacall's belly button. While extremely seductive for the time, it shows a certain restraint that would become characteristic of Bacall's style. Nothing is overtly sexual and her other costumes continue this look. They seem inspired by a man's wardrobe, including the patterns. There are stripes galore, from the robe she wears when she sits on Steve's lap to the matching blouse and skirt she appears in while helping members of the Resistance. This look reflected the war years, a time that often meant making the most of one bolt of fabric. The hint at masculinity helped reinforce the ideal Hawksian woman, someone who could go toe-to-toe with any man.

Not only did *To Have and Have Not* set the stage for a lasting love affair, it also launched the style of Lauren Bacall. Unlike others in Hollywood, hers was a quiet glamour. She emanated sex appeal through her natural beauty, her feline grace, her strength. Her aspirational style was also accessible because of the simplicity of the things she wore. Two costumes from *To Have and Have Not* continue to inspire. Bacall's gingham suit has been replicated often—from major houses to retro reproductions lines. But Anderson's black satin gown is so special that no one has been able to copy it successfully.

Even Lauren's look has been in-

Bacall's wardrobe is filled with stripes, including her well-known "You know how to whistle, don't you, Steve?" robe. (Everett Collection)

fluential in fashion, her hair and makeup emulated in marketing campaigns with models doing their best to lower their chins and gaze seductively into the camera. No one, however, can match the authenticity of Bacall. Her smart clothing choices were true to her, showed elements of strength, and always seemed sensual rather than sexual. Her style inspiration lives on.

Claire Trevor is dressed to kill as femme fatale Helen Grayle. (Greenbriar Collection)

Murder, My Sweet

Premiere: December 9, 1944
Director: Edward Dmytryk
Costume designer: Edward Stevenson
Studio: RKO

There's something about the dead silence of an office building at night ... not quite real. The traffic down below was something that didn't have anything to do with me.

So begin the adventures of Philip Marlowe in *Murder, My Sweet*. Raymond Chandler's alley-prowling private eye has been played by many actors, most memorably Humphrey Bogart, but also by Robert Montgomery, James Garner, and even Elliot Gould. Dick Powell, however, portrayed him first.

Murder, My Sweet opens with Marlowe being grilled by the police and starting to share the story of his search for missing singer Velma Valento. RKO director Edward Dmytryk, who soon would suffer noir in his own life as a result of the Hollywood blacklist, helped to shape the look and feel of the genre. *Murder, My Sweet* contains all the essential elements—the voiceover narration, the dominant darkness and atmospheric lighting, violence so severe it was shown with special effects, and, of course, the gorgeous and greedy femme fatale. Claire Trevor played this part so well that she, too, helped define the genre. Along with costume designer Edward Stevenson, she set a standard in style that would influence both film and fashion.

Raymond Chandler enjoyed a big 1944 as Hollywood optioned his novels, one by one, as source material for some of the best in film noir. He had seen a steady stream of his novels published, beginning with *The Big Sleep* in 1939, followed by *Farewell, My Lovely*—the story that would become *Murder, My Sweet*—in 1940, *The High Window* in 1942, and *The Lady in the Lake* in 1943. He also wrote screenplays, adapting James M. Cain's *Double Indemnity* and crafting an original screenplay for *The Blue Dahlia*.

Whereas Dashiell Hammett's detective Sam Spade navigated within the dark side of San

Francisco, Chandler's Philip Marlowe, featured in all seven of his novels, traveled the less-than-sunny side of Los Angeles. The city proved an important character in his work and background for the style of *Murder, My Sweet*. The audience experiences the sprawl of the city as the private eye moves from one neighborhood to the next, from his office within the older high-rise buildings of Hollywood to the Sunset Tower Hotel where Jules Amthor (Otto Kruger) lives to the Cocoanut Beach Club situated on the edge of Santa Monica Bay. As Marlowe, Powell pounds the pavement to track down stolen jewelry in addition to a missing girl and gets pounded by adversaries along the way.

In the 1930s Powell had shone as one of Warner Bros.' brightest stars. Unlike contract players James Cagney and Edward G. Robinson who gained prominence in the studio's signature gangster pictures, Powell delighted audiences in musicals like *42nd Street* (1933). That movie became such a massive hit that *Gold Diggers of 1933* and *Footlight Parade* followed the same year. Powell's success led to his typecasting as a baby-faced crooner in productions through the remainder of the decade.

Dick Powell and Claire Trevor define the dark, sexy style of film noir in *Murder, My Sweet*. (Everett Collection)

In moving from musicals to murder, Powell transformed his career playing tough private eye Philip Marlowe. (Everett Collection)

He moved to Paramount in 1940 hoping for different roles but failed to escape his past and found himself singing in musicals once again. While at the studio, he sought the lead in *Double Indemnity*, but director Billy Wilder couldn't see it. "Well, look, Dick," said Wilder, "I can take a comedian and make this picture. But I can't take a singer."

Undeterred, Powell tried again at RKO, which had optioned Chandler's novel *Farewell, My Lovely*. Some of the story had been used for plot points in another detective picture, *The Falcon Takes Over* (1942), but studio head Charles Koerner and producer Adrian Scott saw the value in the entirety of the book, particularly the character of Marlowe. Edward Dmytryk, who had success directing B pictures, was given the green light for the film, and Dick went knocking on Dmytryk's door. Now nearly forty, Powell had lost his baby face and acquired more toughness.

"He was a lot taller and huskier and more masculine than he looked in those Warners musicals," Dmytryk remembered. "We decided to try him. That was the best thing we ever did." To avoid confusion the studio changed the title of *Farewell, My Lovely* to *Murder, My Sweet* so audiences wouldn't expect another musical from the former song-and-dance man.

In retrospect, the name change seems unnecessary. Powell put on a trench coat and fedora and successfully inhabited the world of the hard-drinking and often obstinate detective. He performed so well that he won over Chandler himself, who, according to *Los Angeles Times* reporter Dennis McClellan, "considered Powell's Philip Marlowe closer to his own conception of his fictional private eye than that portrayed by Humphrey Bogart."

Film critic Karl Krug declared, "In all the history of Hollywood, no actor that I can remember has made the transition from 'pretty boy' type to melodramatic hard guy with quite the success of Dick Powell."

In contrast to Powell, Claire Trevor seemed right at home in the world of noir. Prior to *Murder, My Sweet*, she had already proved herself a skillful actress, even while playing bad girls and prostitutes in movies like William Wyler's crime drama *Dead End* (1937) and John Ford's western *Stagecoach* (1939). Trevor would become so

Trevor's high fashion from *Murder, My Sweet* often pushed the limits of the Production Code, including this gown that used sheer fabric to protect her plunging decolletage. (Everett Collection)

dominant in the genre that she earned the title "the queen of film noir," according to biographer Derek Sculthorpe and others.

In addition to being a celebrated actress, Trevor became a trendsetter. Clothes had always been a passion. She was plugged into fashion from an early age thanks to her parents. Her mother was a skilled dressmaker who outfitted Claire in beautiful clothes. Her father, a talented tailor, ran a successful shop on Fifth Avenue in Manhattan.

"[He] was the best custom tailor in New York," Trevor remembered, "and his clients were the heads of top businesses." Trevor's family inspired her desire to be a fashion designer, and she studied at Smith College focusing on suit design like her father. When the stock market crashed in 1929, so did her family's fortune. By this time she also had attended the prestigious American

Academy of Dramatic Arts—alumni include Rosalind Russell and Spencer Tracy—so the theater became her direction, and she modeled to help pay the bills. Through it all, fashion would remain an important part of her life.

Like Ginger Rogers and other stylish actresses of the age, Claire Trevor endorsed a line of sewing patterns. Her name also appeared on a range of products, from Max Factor lipstick to Woodbury cold cream. Claire frequently made her way into beauty columns, where she was quoted giving her secrets, and she wrote articles on beauty and fashion for newspapers and film magazines. While beloved for being a trendsetter, she also became a role model for women in the 1930s. *Screenland* magazine decided that "[Claire Trevor] personifies the self-reliant modern

Sex was always a part of the strategy for greedy femme fatale Helen Grayle. (Everett Collection)

girl." She was so popular that studio PR departments regularly featured her costumes in the pages of *Photoplay* before and after her movie premieres.

Murder, My Sweet lifted Trevor in both popularity and fashion influence, due in part to her collaboration with RKO costume designer Edward Stevenson. Stevenson is not as well known as others, such as Edith Head or Orry-Kelly, but he made significant contributions to the costume design of noir. With vast experience in Hollywood's major studios, he made the biggest impact in the films of RKO. He first assisted Bernard Newman (*Top Hat*) from 1935 to 1938 and then replaced him as head of costume design after Newman left. Stevenson's work in the 1940s included *Citizen Kane, Journey into Fear* (1943), and later in the decade, *Out of the Past*. With *Murder, My Sweet*, Edward Stevenson helped to define the look of the femme fatale.

Trevor's startlingly sexy entrance as Helen Grayle communicates the character without a

Edward Stevenson (far right) discusses costumes with Irene Dunne during production of *Joy of Living* (1938). (Everett Collection)

word via a white dress and a lot of leg. Unlike other aspects of the film, this costume and others did not result from either the novel or the script. The book described a "rather plain" dress of a "pale greenish blue" and the script asked for shorts. Trevor rejected both because she thought they failed to convey the intrinsic sexuality of this femme fatale. She then proceeded to design the now famously revealing white dress. The key elements were a peek-a-boo section of skin beneath the bodice and a skirt split all the way up to her hip. Her legs were highlighted further with strappy sandals that wrapped around her ankles. Because the dress was needed for the first day of filming, Stevenson stayed up all the night before to make it to Trevor's specifications.

The public went wild over the provocative introduction of the picture's femme fatale. (Everett Collection)

The next morning on set was frantic. Claire was literally sewn into the costume and ended up having to do her own makeup, including body makeup. The slit in the skirt traveled so high that while shooting one scene, Dmytryk directed Dick Powell to push a table in front of a seated Trevor. Not surprisingly, the public went wild for this look. Trevor remembered her husband's reaction to her leggy introduction. "He still hasn't gotten over the whistles and stamping that went up when *Murder, My Sweet* was shown at his [military] base!" she said. The studio loved the public's reaction and included the dress in a fashion show to promote the film. The design was so popular, it would inspire future costumes.

Trevor participated in sports ranging from tennis to surfing and gained a reputation for fitness. As a result, she could wear almost anything. That said, at a petite 5'3" she wore costumes designed to add the appearance of height—including the two gowns in *Murder, My Sweet*. When Helen invites Marlowe to the Cocoanut Beach Club, she wears a glamorous floor-length gown that mixes sheer with sequins. Stevenson used sheer fabric to fashion the long sleeves and to protect her plunging décolletage from violating the Production Code. Then he used a large peacock brooch to hide shoulder pads that were slightly visible underneath. Even her hair adds height with victory rolls teased up high. Stevenson accessorized the gown with an oversized ostrich feather muff that doubles as a purse carrying Marlowe's money. This costume, more than any other in her wardrobe, flaunts Helen's wealth and stands in sharp contrast to the more sensible styles favored by her stepdaughter, Ann (Anne Shirley).

For a more intimate moment with Marlowe, Helen emerges from the shadows of her Malibu beach house wearing a trench coat, her long blonde hair tumbling over her shoulders. The trench had become a staple in film noir, including for Powell in *Murder, My Sweet*. Women wore them too. Trench coats helped to give an air of mystery to Greta Garbo in *Woman of Affairs* (1928) and to Marlene Dietrich in *Morocco*. The costume also signified strength of character. Femme fatale Helen conveys both mystery and strength when she comes face to face with Marlowe. Her strategy is seduction, and she takes off the trench to reveal lacy lingerie, teasing the detective with her body before wrapping herself in a fancy floor-length robe.

The other gown Trevor wears in the film—one that became highly influential—appears in the final showdown. It's the perfect look for "big league blondes," as Ann calls Helen in a confrontation, "beautiful, expensive babes who know what they've got." Stevenson again designed a long-sleeved, floor-length gown, streamlined and sophisticated. Rather than the almost excessive details of the earlier dress, this gown is sleek with a strong-shouldered, bishop-sleeved top striped

Helen reveals her true identity and motivations in a strong floor-length gown striped with sequins. (Everett Collection)

Trevor's white dress would influence the style of many femmes fatales to come—from Lana Turner in *The Postman Always Rings Twice* to Sharon Stone in *Basic Instinct*. (Everett Collection)

with sequins. Its V neckline further elongates Claire, whose hair is piled high on her head to add height. It proved to be a strong look that captures the essence of the femme fatale as she reveals her true identity and motivations to Marlowe.

One of Trevor's early theatrical ambitions had been to play Lady Macbeth, so it's natural that she played femmes fatales and intrigantes so well. "Her run of peerless '40s portrayals helped shape the image of the genre: alluring beauty that proves fatal," said Sculthorpe.

Claire may not be as well known today as contemporaries Lana Turner and Ava Gardner, but she made a significant impact on both film and fashion. The white dress she wears in the opening of *Murder, My Sweet* influenced costume design for other femmes fatales—from Turner's white wardrobe in *The Postman Always Rings Twice* to Sharon Stone's short white dress in *Basic Instinct* (1992). The peek-a-boo design detail of Trevor's costume would reemerge in Marilyn Monroe's pink dress in the noir *Niagara* (1953). In addition, Claire's two black sequined gowns appear in various incarnations in fashion, including on the red carpet for the Oscars. The trench coat she wore would cloak Ava Gardner in *The Killers*, inspiring women to add the trench to their own wardrobes.

Missing singer Velma Valento might have been described as "cute as lace pants" in *Murder, My Sweet*, but she became all greed and glamour when she hid behind the name Helen Grayle thanks to the transformational abilities and style of Claire Trevor.

The broad-shouldered mink coat in *Mildred Pierce* is signature Joan Crawford style. (Everett Collection)

Mildred Pierce

Premiere: September 28, 1945
Director: Michael Curtiz
Costume designer: Milo Anderson
Studio: Warner Bros.

Inside a beautiful beach house, six gunshots ring out in the night and a man in a tuxedo utters his last word before dying: "Mildred." Although that seems to be a suggestion as to the murderer, no one sees who emptied every chamber of a gun into the target, and the mystery of *Mildred Pierce* begins.

James M. Cain's novel and director Michael Curtiz' vision made *Mildred Pierce* unlike any other film noir of the era. A woman rather than a man serves as the main character, and it is this woman who suffers for her love of a femme fatale and the dark side of the American dream. Joan Crawford not only masters the character of Mildred but embodies her, bringing every ounce of her own life experience and lessons of resilience to the role. She also helped make the movie one of the most important from a standpoint of style, with Milo Anderson's costumes continuing to influence fashion. For all these reasons, the "femme" noir *Mildred Pierce* transcends the genre as an essential film of the 1940s.

Cain's novel *Mildred Pierce*, the story of a middle-class mother of two who struggles to support her family during the Great Depression, was published in 1941. Survival is not enough, however. Her materialistic daughter demands to be spoiled and enjoy the highest social standing, so Mildred moves from waiting tables to launching several successful restaurants in order to satisfy her. What makes Mildred modern is that her ambitions from her business to her bedroom seem like those more often associated with a man.

The Production Code Administration had found plenty to object to in the novel—but then Warner Bros. producer Jerry Wald and director Michael Curtiz added murder to the story. They followed a formula that worked when adapting Cain's *Double Indemnity* and Raymond Chandler's *Farewell, My Lovely* to the screen: Start with a murder and then tell the story in flashback. In doing so, Mildred became the put-upon protagonist suffering from the femme fatale that is her snobbish, selfish, and self-centered daughter Veda (Ann Blyth).

In many ways, Joan Crawford was the only woman who should have played the part of Mildred Pierce. Her own life could have been the basis for another noir. Born Lucille LeSueur, she survived a difficult childhood. At one point, poverty forced the family of three—mother, brother, and little Lucille—to work and live in the back room of a laundry that smelled so bad it would haunt her life. She had little education; most of her schools demanded physical labor as tuition, so hours spent scrubbing floors outnumbered those committed to studying. A miserable mother who attracted the worst of men added to Lucille's miseries; even the nicest "daddy" among them abused her. This broken childhood would cause her to spend much of her life searching desperately for love. "I believe my greatest weakness was I needed love too much," Joan told her biographer Charlotte Chandler.

Dancing saved her. It began as a passion and became her career. Lucille danced at venues across the country as Billie Cassin, taking the last name of her mother's second husband. She finally made it to New York City where MGM producer and talent scout Harry Rapf discovered her in the second row of a chorus line.

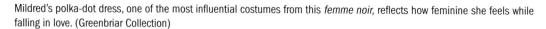

Mildred's polka-dot dress, one of the most influential costumes from this *femme noir,* reflects how feminine she feels while falling in love. (Greenbriar Collection)

Milo Anderson's suspender dress is eerily similar to one Adrian designed for Katharine Hepburn in *Woman of the Year* (1942). (Everett Collection)

"I danced where I wanted to go in life," Joan said. "I danced to Hollywood. I danced into the arms of MGM." Even after she signed with the studio and was christened Joan Crawford, she continued to dance in contests at the Cocoanut Grove, Café Montmartre, and other celebrity-filled nightclubs in Los Angeles. She won almost every contest she entered. She had learned from the best publicity men in the business and astutely understood the value of self-promotion.

Joan's strategy landed her the starring role in *Our Dancing Daughters* (1928), and so began the ascent of one of the biggest stars of Hollywood's golden era. In *Dream of Love* (1928) she was dressed by MGM's new head costume designer, Adrian, and together they formed one of the greatest star-designer partnerships. They helped to define the glamour of the studio and the style of the 1930s in productions like *Possessed* (1931), *Grand Hotel* (1932), and *The Women* (1939). *Letty Lynton* (1932) in particular made an enormous impact on fashion, with thousands of copies of one of her gowns sold in department stores. With that dress as well as many others, Adrian exaggerated Crawford's naturally broad shoulders to minimize her hips and waist. The world went mad for the look, and the strong-shouldered style would soon be a defining feature

Above: Crawford had many opinions about the look of Mildred Pierce, which posed a challenge to director Michael Curtiz (left). Below: Crawford's struggles in life allowed her to understand a lot about the character. (Both photos, GKB Collection)

of 1940s clothing both on and off the screen.

A popular saying emerged from MGM that "[Norma] Shearer was the productions, [Greta] Garbo supplied the art, and Joan Crawford made the money to pay for both." Even so, Joan among others earned the label "box office poison" in a 1938 article by the Independent Theatre Owners of America. In addition, Joan grew to resent the parts MGM offered her through the early 1940s. While it's popularly believed that Louis B. Mayer forced Crawford out of the studio, many sources say this is not the case. Instead, Joan asked to be released her from her contract.

"I felt I had something to give, and they gave me a couple of stinkers, so I just said: 'Thank you, but no.'" According to those close to her, including ex-husband Douglas Fairbanks, Jr., Mayer ultimately did as she asked, but he imposed a penalty of $50,000. Joan then packed up her dressing room and, true to form, cleaned it top to bottom. No one bothered to celebrate the massive contributions she made to the studio before she left. She just drove off the lot. But the survivor drove away with Lew Wasserman as her agent and on to a new contract at Warner Bros. only days later.

Happy as she was to have a new home studio, Crawford didn't care for its initial offerings. In fact, she refused so many projects that she asked frustrated studio head Jack Warner to place her "off salary" until something suitable came along. Finally, something did—the

adaptation of Cain's novel *Mildred Pierce*. Wald wanted Crawford from the start, but Curtiz wasn't so sure. She had a reputation for being difficult and had grown accustomed to the glamour MGM had offered. Mildred wasn't a glamour part. However, Joan felt a connection with the character and wanted the part so badly she offered to do a screen test to prove herself.

"The role was a delight to me because it rescued me from what was known at MGM as the Joan Crawford formula," she said. "I had become so hidden in clothes and sets that nobody could tell whether I had talent or not."

Curtiz brought preconceived notions to the set, and day one forced the first of many showdowns. Joan remembered the scene vividly: "I went down to Sears Roebuck on my own and bought the kind of housedresses I thought Mildred would wear. When I arrived on the set for wardrobe tests, Mr. Curtiz walked over to me, shouting, 'You and your Adrian shoulder pads! This stinks!' And he ripped the dress from neck to hem. 'Mr. Curtiz,' I sobbed, 'I bought this dress this morning for $2.98. There are no shoulder pads!'"

Crawford might not have been wearing shoulder pads that day, but she clearly expected them in her wardrobe. And so, as Wald would describe it, "the battle of the shoulder pads began. And lipstick. And hair."

The character of Mildred was a mother and a working woman, so the vision was always that she look as natural as possible. Though Crawford was still glamorous in the movie, especially

Despite the Curtiz order forbidding Milo Anderson to use shoulder pads in the costumes, the design detail is absolutely everywhere in *Mildred Pierce*. (Top photo, Greenbriar Collection; center and bottom photos, Everett Collection)

111

as Mildred achieves some success, her makeup was distinctly downplayed.

"I did away with those long eyelashes, I scrubbed off that wide curved mouth," Curtiz told columnist Harrison Carroll when he visited the set. Co-star Lee Patrick, who played Maggie Biederhof, remembered the director constantly going over to Joan and "mussing up her hair and changing her makeup." Crawford may have resisted, but she ended up looking stunning in *Mildred Pierce*. With her encouragement of close-ups—or perhaps insistence—Curtiz and cine-matographer Ernest Haller captured every flicker of emotion on that perfect face.

Curtiz might have set a goal to deglamorize Joan, but it's clear she battled back. Fortunately, she was in costume designer Milo Anderson's capable hands. Dressing MGM's former star was not, however, a dream come true for Anderson.

"When she came to Warner's for *Mildred Pierce*, she was a monster," he later remembered. "Whatever you suggested, she fought tooth and nail. She hated the housedresses and waitress uniforms at the beginning of the picture. We had many expensive-looking clothes for the latter part of the film, but she didn't like those either because they weren't gaudy like the clothes she'd had at MGM.... I did everything I could to accommodate her, but at the time, I knew that the director Michael Curtiz wanted the clothes simple and, above all, no shoulder pads!"

Even with all that forbidding, shoulder pads are everywhere in the costumes. Everywhere. In fact, *Mildred Pierce* solidifies the look that Crawford and Adrian started in the 1930s. The pads are big as life in her opening outfit: a broad-shouldered mink chubby with a matching hat that is quintessential Joan Crawford style. In addition to being famous for this fur, the film was and continues to be celebrated for its suits—skirt suits in different fabrics, colors, and design details. There were stand-up collars, built-in scarves, peplums, and more. Strong shoulders remain consistent throughout, the very thing Curtiz sought to avoid.

Sometimes Crawford's ability to act is overlooked because of her dramatic style. Fortunately, Curtiz and cinematographer Ernest Haller captured every flicker of emotion on her perfect face. (Left photo, GKB Collection; right photo, Everett Collection)

The pin-striped skirt suit ranks as the most influential of the *Mildred Pierce* costumes and continues to be seen in career wear. (Everett Collection)

Her entire collection of suits proved to be influential, but the navy pin-striped suit she wears at the peak of Mildred's success has had the strongest impact on fashion. The slim, fitted jacket and pencil skirt, supremely stylish in their simplicity, embodied the wartime need to conserve fabric. To vary the looks of Mildred's suits further, Anderson accessorized them with sparkling brooches and hats, which remained popular because they were among the few things not rationed during the war. Anderson also paired her suits with ankle-strap pumps, shoes that have become associated with Crawford's signature style.

When Mildred first goes out with Wally Fay (Jack Carson), she's somewhat businesslike in a black-and-white suspender dress that is similar to one Adrian had designed for Katharine Hepburn in *Woman of the Year* (1942). Mildred's visits to the Malibu beach house of Monte Beragon (Zachary Scott) bring out a different side of her wardrobe.

When things are sunny for Mildred and she falls in love with Monte, Anderson dresses her in a flowing, white long-sleeved dress with polka dots. An ocean swim offers the opportunity to show off Crawford's figure in a white two-piece bathing suit. Monte says that he'd "need a police siren" rather than a mere whistle when he sees her, and that's not an exaggeration. Swimsuits, let alone a risqué two-piece, were not common on-screen during the 1930s and '40s due to the Production Code. Further, Crawford was just over forty when she made *Mildred Pierce*, and she looked as incredible as ever. For an actress already feeling the bite of getting older in Hollywood, likely one of the reasons she hadn't been getting good parts at MGM, this had to be a moment in the movie she savored.

Despite Crawford's misery behind the scenes, her publicity for the picture was quite different. With the film still in production, columnist Harold Heffernan reported, "Joan Crawford in *Mildred Pierce* says she hasn't been dressed so elegantly in five years." The positive press would soon move beyond her costumes. Praise for her performance in this pivotal role strengthened into Oscar predictions by some Hollywood insiders, including Hedda Hopper. Crawford would go on to win the film's only Academy Award despite multiple nominations, including for Best Picture. Shockingly, Joan skipped the ceremony at Grauman's Chinese Theatre and remained in bed—sick, so she said—wearing what the press described as "a fluffy blue nightgown and a coffee-colored negligee" as she heard her named called on the radio. Curtiz, not nominated himself, delivered the gold statuette to Joan at her home. Friends such as Van Johnson and Ann Blyth also dropped in with their own congratulations for the Best Actress of the year.

Crawford would be nominated for two more Academy Awards in her career, and both were for films noir—*Possessed* (1947) and *Sudden Fear* (1952). Not only does this attention show the significance of the genre, it also marks a transition in Joan's career. She had skillfully moved from the party girl of the 1920s and '30s to the powerful, independent woman of the 1940s and beyond. *Mildred Pierce* became that pivot point, and her wardrobe from the film continued to influence both costume design and fashion. It dominated Sean Young's style in *Blade Runner* (1982) and served as a reference for productions such as *Hollywoodland* and *The Black Dahlia* (both 2006).

Mildred's navy pin-striped suit can still be seen in some form in almost every career-geared wardrobe. For many reasons, *Mildred Pierce* was a milestone. Beyond the melodrama of Cain and Curtiz, the film noir reflected the ever-changing opportunities for women as professionals and entrepreneurs and showed audiences a classic working woman's wardrobe that continues to inspire.

A mere whistle isn't reaction enough when Crawford steps out in a white two-piece swim suit. (Everett Collection)

The Year of Transition
1946

U.S. military personnel return on the *Queen Elizab*
(U.S. Navy photo)

Homecoming

Massive activity around military demobilization in 1946 marked the end of the war years and heralded a time of transition in the United States. About 1.5 million personnel returned to America in December 1945 alone, and the military continued to discharge 35,000 people a day through 1946. Because of the number of soldiers coming home, 1946 was also the beginning of the post-war period as the population struggled to settle into the new normal.

The demobilization also brought about tremendous change in the country for women. Most had remained homemakers during the war, and those who did enter the workforce experienced a newfound strength and independence. They proved to society they could do anything a man could do. Many even proved it to themselves. By the time the war ended, women were thriving in their jobs and made up a full third of the workforce. Most wanted to continue. In fact, surveys revealed that 61–85 percent of the women working wanted to stay employed. Even among married women, who everyone assumed would rush back to being homemakers, a whopping 47–68 percent wanted to continue working. This would not be possible. Once soldiers started to return, most women lost their jobs. Some industries were particularly brutal; factories engaged in building aircraft or ships, for example, released women after the war at almost double the rate for men. It was a painful reality of peacetime.

Despite peace, wartime restrictions continued to dictate fashion design for some time. The Civilian Production Administration didn't end rationing instituted by Limitation Order 85 until October 1946—more than a year after the end of the war. It would also take some time before fabric and other material from both America and abroad became available once again to the U.S.

garment industry. As a result, the fashion collections for Fall 1945 and Spring 1946 still reflected the wartime silhouette. Paris designers in particular attempted to soften things a bit more each season, but significant change would not arrive until Christian Dior's "New Look" in February 1947. Women would have to wait to indulge in hyper-feminine designs.

Men found a source for their style outside the fashion industry: their military apparel. Peacetime wardrobes were filled with familiar white T-shirts and chinos as well as pea coats, bomber jackets, and trench coats, all eventual fashion classics.

For many reasons, 1946 was a huge year for Hollywood. Weekly attendance was at an all-time high. "The surge actually accelerated immediately after the war, thanks to millions of returning servicemen, increased courtship activity, the easing of wartime restrictions, and a generally upbeat populace with both time and wartime savings on their hands," reported historian Thomas Schatz. The Motion Picture Association of America calculated weekly attendance at 95–100 million people, which resulted in the studios doubling their profits in 1946. The boom peaked at the end of the year with $1.7 billion in box office.

Another reason for that big box office was the quality of 1946 films. Classics like *The Best Years of Our Lives*, *It's a Wonderful Life*, *My Darling Clementine*, *The Razor's Edge*, and *Duel in the Sun* are just a few of what theaters featured that year. Alongside those offerings were a number of film noir giants. Whereas 1939 is widely considered the greatest year in film, it could be argued that 1946 is the greatest year in film noir. *Gilda*, *The Killers*, *The Postman Always Rings Twice*, *The Big Sleep*,

The Best Years of Our Lives was the biggest box-office hit of 1946 and a critical success, winning seven Academy Awards including Best Picture. (Greenbriar Collection)

Faith Domergue arrives on the *Young Widow* set and steps out in 1946 style. (Everett Collection)

Notorious, The Blue Dahlia, The Strange Love of Martha Ivers, The Stranger, and *Deception* all had premieres in calendar year 1946.

Screenwriter and *LIFE* magazine film critic D.M. Marshman wrote: "Whoever went to the movies with any regularity in 1946 was caught in the midst of Hollywood's profound post-war affection for morbid drama. From January through December, deep shadows, clutching hands, exploding revolvers, sadistic villains, and heroines tormented with deeply rooted diseases of the mind, flashed across the screen in a panting display of psychoneuroses, unsublimated sex, and murder most foul. Apparently delighted to pay good money for having their pants scared off, movie-goers flocked in record numbers to these spectacles."

Because many films noir were in production the last year of the war, these movies still reflect the more streamlined silhouette in the costumes. Despite the restrictions, this roster of pictures boasts memorable and influential designs, such as Rita Hayworth's strapless number from *Gilda* and Ava Gardner's one-shouldered gown from *The Killers*. Fashion designers know these costumes well and invoke them again and again in their collections. The inspiration of costumes from 1946, including the look of the hair and makeup, make it a year from the past that's very much part of the present. It's a peak year in film history thanks to millions of returning servicemen and the zenith of film noir style.

One of the most famous dresses in Hollywood history: Rita Hayworth's "Put the Blame on Mame" gown from *Gilda*. (Everett Collection)

Gilda

Premiere: February 14, 1946
Director: Charles Vidor
Costume designer: Jean Louis
Studio: Columbia

Some movies are so sexy they sizzle no matter how often they're viewed, and Charles Vidor's *Gilda* tops this list. There's a heat in it—a sultriness that permeates everything from the production and costume design to the dialogue and the way the actors look at each other. The film is set in Argentina at the end of World War II and centers on a woman with a past caught in a love triangle with a gambler who was once her lover and his boss who is now her husband. Every interaction between these characters is taut with tension.

There's something new to experience with each viewing of this film thanks to its star, Rita Hayworth, a leading lady capable of making mere mortals swoon. From the moment her character appears with a flirtatious flip of her hair and seductive smile in answer to a question—"Gilda, are you decent?"—she slips effortlessly into the role of intrigante.

Although Hayworth had crept into the public's consciousness in the rugged aviation picture *Only Angels Have Wings* and established herself as a dancer in bright Columbia musicals like *You Were Never Lovelier* (1942) with Fred Astaire and *Cover Girl* (1944) with Gene Kelly, *Gilda* secured Rita's star in the heavens.

Rita Hayworth started life in Brooklyn as Margarita Cansino. Her mother, Volga, had been a Ziegfeld Girl and her father, Eduardo, owned a dance studio and taught the likes of Jean Harlow and James Cagney. Margarita had danced and performed in public with her father from an early age, but this talent failed to transfer to the big screen. Her lackluster presence caused the studio that discovered her, 20th Century Fox, to drop her after only a few pictures. Stylist Helen Hunt and first husband Eddie Judson (Rita had five, including Orson Welles) encouraged her to undergo painful electrolysis to change her hairline and to lighten her hair from black to auburn

The character of Gilda is introduced with a flip of her hair while she wears this more innocent dressing gown. (GKB Collection)

to change her image. These changes did indeed transform Rita Cansino—studio head Harry Cohn brought her back as Rita Hayworth and signed her to a contract with Columbia Pictures.

Several respected talents aligned with the making of *Gilda*, including Columbia's head costume designer Jean Louis and cinematographer Rudolph Maté. These two pros allowed Hayworth to shine bright. Maté was a star in his own right, known for his lush and beautiful cinematography both in and out of film noir. Hitchcock's *Foreign Correspondent* (1940), Ernst Lubitsch's *To Be or Not to Be* (1942), and later Orson Welles' *The Lady from Shanghai* (again starring Rita) all feature his camera work. Maté would go on to direct some of the best in film noir, including the classic *D.O.A.*, released in 1950. Maté's work produces a depth to black and white that is unmatched by most, and he is revered as one of the great cinematographers.

Maté operated the camera for Rita's screen test at Columbia, and his approach to shooting her helped studio head Harry Cohn see her potential. Maté would be a perfect partner on *Gilda* with director Vidor, whose intimate framing seems to have influenced later movies like *A Place in the Sun* (1951). Characters often are shown in silhouette or even in the dark, and some close-ups almost make the audience feel like they are intruding.

Contributions to the visual appeal of *Gilda* also came courtesy of costume designer Jean Louis. Louis designed some of the most stunning wardrobes on film, including clothes for the studio's biggest stars Rita Hayworth, Judy Holliday, and Kim Novak. After he moved to Universal, he worked with Doris Day in *Pillow Talk* and Lana Turner in *Imitation of Life* (both 1959). Louis is also famous for his designs for the stage, such as the nude illusion gowns he made for Marlene Dietrich when she performed her Las Vegas cabaret act and for Marilyn Monroe when she sang "Happy Birthday, Mr. President" to John F. Kennedy at Madison Square Garden.

Like many costume designers, Jean Louis began his career in fashion at two of the best couturiers in the world—Agnès-Drecoll in Paris and then Hattie Carnegie in New York. Louis would later close his career in fashion with a successful line of his own, which was sold through his Beverly Hills boutique and in luxury department stores.

Of all these successes, his work in film made him legendary through one celebrated design after another, including in film noir. Like previous Columbia head costume designers Robert Kalloch and mentor Travis Banton before him, Louis brought an elegance to the studio that belied its origins on "Poverty Row." Even in the fabric-rationed years of World War II, audiences could count on Jean's costumes to be alluring.

The wardrobe for Gilda epitomizes glamour and extravagance. Hayworth had grown in popularity with the public, including as a pinup girl during the war, so Columbia invested heavily in dressing its rising star and "Love Goddess." Just two of her furs—a chinchilla evening wrap and an ermine cloak—cost $100,000.

While her twenty-nine costumes included two tailored suits that were *de rigueur* for the 1940s, the film is best known for its gorgeous gowns. One, in particular, has become iconic: the strapless black satin dress she wears to strip tease while singing "Put the Blame on Mame." With a design inspired by John Singer Sargent's painting *Madame X*, Louis captured the mood and mystery of the portrait for the character of Gilda. Audiences were in awe because it seemed to defy gravity; no matter how much Rita moved in her dance, the dress did not. The gown was a marvel of engineering in addition to beauty. Louis revealed, "Inside there was a harness like you put on a horse. We put grosgrain under the bust with darts and three stays, one in the center, two on the sides. Then we molded plastic soft-

The strapless "Put the Blame on Mame" gown was an achievement in engineering as much as it was in design. (GKB Collection)

There's heat in every scene with Hayworth and co-star Glenn Ford. (Everett Collection)

ened over a gas flame and shaped around the top of the dress. No matter how she moved, the dress did not fall down."

With this costume and the others in the movie, Louis did what all great designers do: He made the star look her absolute best. Even the 5'6" Hayworth had her physical flaws. "Rita had a good body. It wasn't difficult to dress her," Jean recalled. "She was very thin-limbed—the legs were thin, the arms long and thin, and she had beautiful hands. But [her] body was thick. She also had a belly then." The belly he describes was courtesy of a recent pregnancy, so Louis included a faux side tie in the "Mame" gown to add distracting detail and help conceal her midsection. Another gown in the film has ruching around the middle that offers much the same effect. Several gowns bare Hayworth's shoulders, drawing the audience's eye upward. Still other dresses were accessorized with wide belts that help define her waist, including one embellished with studs paired with a matching cuff that make Gilda look like a warrior ready for battle. And, of course, each costume was fit to perfection to flatter Hayworth's figure.

The Production Code restricted costume designers in many ways. Nothing could hint at nudity, and the administration could prohibit any costumes they found too suggestive or revealing. Cleavage (or even the shadow of it) was objectionable as was the sight of a woman's belly button. Yet even with censors attempting to dictate design, Louis' gowns are sublimely sensual. The gown Rita wears in the "Amado Mio" number is a perfect illustration of Louis working around the Code. The two-piece design is backless, bares much of her midriff, and features a skirt that resembles a sarong, yet its long sleeves and floor length make her seem much more covered than she really is. Also, as with the design for "Mame," Jean included high side slits that are largely hidden until Hayworth dances. Only then do they reveal and highlight her lovely legs.

In the 1940s, films were at the forefront of fashion. The production process meant movies were conceived about a year before their release, and so costume designers had to be ahead of trends. In fact, they more often set them. This was the case with the strapless "Mame" gown, which Jean described as "bolder and sexier than film designs of the time." Banton had created a strapless gown for film two years earlier, but Louis' look for *Gilda* captured the imagination of audiences at the time and inspired a trend. The design's popularity would continue well into the 1950s and beyond.

"It was the most famous dress I ever made," Jean declared. As testimony to this, his custom copy of the "Mame" dress has been included in two Metropolitan Museum of Art exhibitions, one curated by Diana Vreeland in 1974 and another in 2019.

It also remains highly influential in fashion. "Every designer has copied that gown," insists Nolan Miller, who counts costume design for television's *Dynasty* among his credits. Award show red carpets provide visible proof—precious few events don't feature at least one gown owing its origin to Jean Louis' creation.

As head of costume design, Louis also supervised the men's wardrobes. Glenn Ford's character, Johnny Farrell, goes through a significant emotional evolution, especially early in the film, and those changes are reflected in his costumes. The audience meets the gambler on his hands and knees with messy hair and an ill-fitting tweed jacket and pants. Still clad in the jacket, which sports a patch pocket rather than a more sophisticated welt breast pocket, he adds a gaudy striped tie on his first visit to Ballin Mundson's casino. But as soon as Farrell is brought into the fold and made casino manager, he assembles a custom-made wardrobe—first a tuxedo, followed by dou-

Jean Louis used several techniques to hide Hayworth's midsection and define her waist. He accessorized this goddess gown with a wide belt and a long embellished coat. (Both photos, Everett Collection)

ble-breasted, chalked-striped suits accented with pocket squares. Even his pajamas are tailored to perfection.

Mundson's clothing is consistently elegant yet sinister—an assortment of tuxedos and dark suits paired with sophisticated ties that show off his wealth. And when going out, he adds evening coats and even a cape along with his character's signature accessory—a cane concealing a knife within. Jean didn't miss a detail in the costume design as he revealed the film's characters to the audience.

Such talents working together to create *Gilda* made the movie a phenomenon—an immediate box-office hit for Columbia and a career boost for Hayworth, who became beloved by men and women all over the world. She was already a favorite glamour girl, but playing Gilda turned her into a siren. Servicemen returning to America in 1946 "flocked to the film

The "Amado Mio" gown danced around the Production Code with its daring two-piece design. (GKB Collection)

to see their wartime pinup come to life," according to Hayworth biographer Barbara Leaming. Co-star Glenn Ford confessed his own affection for Hayworth years later, which explains the strength of their on-screen chemistry. But Rita understood all that made *Gilda* possible and believed that precious little had to do with the real (and painfully shy) Margarita Cansino. Jean Louis' celebrated costumes, particularly the "Mame" gown, transformed her into a temptress. They also helped to create a lasting legacy for the film, for fashion, and—whether she liked it or not—for Hayworth. She famously said, "Men fell in love with Gilda, but they wake up with me." That may be true, but it's hard to believe that anyone was complaining.

This satin strapless gown, one of several with this silhouette in *Gilda*, is paired with a luxurious ermine cloak. (GKB Collection)

Lana Turner stuns in a turban, suit, and heels, making one of the great movie entrances in *The Postman Always Rings Twice*. (Everett Collection)

The Postman Always Rings Twice

Premiere: May 2, 1946
Director: Tay Garnett
Costume designer: Irene
Studio: MGM

Stories of good versus evil go back to earliest literature, and equally timeless is the symbolism in the colors associated with each side. Whether it's Greek tragedy, a Western, or *Star Wars*, antagonists almost always dress in black and protagonists in the purity of white. Odds are audiences don't immediately envision femmes fatales wearing white and certainly not white through the entire movie. Yet this is exactly the color Cora Smith dons in *The Postman Always Rings Twice*. Although Lana Turner arguably is at her most luminous in this film, her nearly all-white wardrobe comes close to stealing the show.

MGM adapted *The Postman Always Rings Twice* from James M. Cain's 1934 bestseller, which had been banned in some locales due to its sadomasochistic sexuality mixed with violence. Cain crafted two other explicit novels that became film noir classics—*Double Indemnity* and *Mildred Pierce*. His two darkest, *The Postman Always Rings Twice* and *Double Indemnity*, feature two very different women. *Double Indemnity*'s Phyllis Dietrichson is evil and cunning to the core. Money motivates her. *Postman*'s Cora may be a femme fatale, but she presents a far more complicated character. Cora seeks security and that's the reason she marries Nick (Cecil Kellaway)—she's a young girl who wants a nice guy to fend off the unwanted advances of men. She doesn't love him, as she confesses to drifter Frank Chambers (John Garfield), although Nick insists that "would come in time." It never does. What starts as a simple affair with a drifter quickly devolves into murder, lust being only one of the sins that drive them.

Postman proved a departure for MGM, the gold standard of movie studios that had produced pictures ranging from the wholesome fare of the Andy Hardy series to sweeping musical extravaganzas. When Turner came to MGM, she appeared in both—*Love Finds Andy Hardy*

(1938) and *Ziegfeld Girl* (1941). *Postman* was also a shift for Lana after starting the 1940s as one of Hollywood's "sweater girls," breaking out as arguably the first in *They Won't Forget* (1937) and then becoming one of the most popular pinups of World War II. By 1945 she remained a major star, but the MGM front office saw her career as bogged down and thought she needed a new image. She would find one in film noir, a genre that worked with the woman Turner had become at age twenty-six and helped make her a Hollywood icon still celebrated decades later.

As one of MGM's most beautiful actresses, Turner became more controversial for her highly publicized life offscreen than for any of her performances on it. Her many relationships with men—including, ultimately, seven husbands—made salacious story lines in newspapers and movie magazines. This reputation would be one of several reasons for her white wardrobe in *The Postman Always Rings Twice*. Her tumultuous private life would hit its lowest point in 1958 when her daughter, Cheryl Crane, stabbed and killed Lana's then-boyfriend, gangster Johnny Stompanato. The *Los Angeles Times* called Turner a hedonist and went even further with their judgment: "Cheryl isn't the juvenile delinquent. Lana is." This widely held opinion of Turner already existed in 1945 when pre-production for *Postman* began. Her reputation combined with the fact that the character Cora was "a villainess who was all the more deadly for her devouring sexuality," as Cheryl Crane phrased it in her book, *Detour: A Hollywood Story*, made an all-white wardrobe for *Postman* seem necessary to camouflage the various crimes.

Postman's director, Tay Garnett, explained: "The white clothing was something that Carey

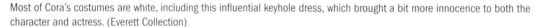

Most of Cora's costumes are white, including this influential keyhole dress, which brought a bit more innocence to both the character and actress. (Everett Collection)

Irene Lentz Gibbons, better known simply as Irene, bridged the gap between fashion and film. (Everett Collection)

[Wilson, the producer] and I thought of. At that time there was a great problem getting a story with that much sex past the censors. We figured that dressing Lana in white somehow made everything she did seem less sensuous… and it somehow took a little of the stigma off of everything she did."

Irene Lentz Gibbons—MGM's head of costume design—had her own reasons for the white wardrobe. Better known to the world as simply Irene, she was a recognized designing talent. After attending the Wolfe School of Design in Los Angeles, she created a line of clothing for her own boutique near USC in 1926. She was so good that stars like Dolores del Río, Carole Lombard, and Marlene Dietrich would sneak out of their respective studios to visit her salon.

With the success of her first store, she moved to a better location on Highland Avenue in 1928, and then to an even better one on Sunset Boulevard in 1929. Irene's powerful reputation led the mighty Bullocks Wilshire department store to ask her to head their new couturier. It was there that del Río first asked Irene to design on-screen costumes as well, starting with those she wore in *Flying Down to Rio*. Other stars would follow suit, and Irene's career in film had begun.

Irene made such an impact in Hollywood on her own that studio head Louis B. Mayer chose her to succeed Adrian as MGM's head of costume design when Adrian retired in 1941. In contrast to colleagues like Helen Rose, Irene preferred designing for black-and-white movies rather than those produced in color. *Postman* proved innovative when Irene decided to restrict the costume design to black and white. In addition to accepting Garnett's justification for Cora's white wardrobe, Irene saw yet another reason to take that approach. Her longtime sketch artist Virginia Fisher said, "The idea was to have a color associated with the character's wardrobe so the color theme of the clothes could work in a movie just like the theme of music in an opera."

The designer also considered the setting of the film. The illicit relationship between Frank and Cora (reportedly carried on by the co-stars offscreen as well) takes place during a southern

Cora's white wardrobe even extended to the ensemble she wears to murder her husband. (Everett Collection)

California summer. The script mentions the Santa Ana winds that carry hot air from the desert, and the couple try to escape the heat with nighttime swims. The white clothes are right for the weather and highlight Lana's suntanned skin. The decision to dominate the character's clothes with white worked on a number of levels and produced some of the most notable costume design in the genre.

Irene created the costumes in an environment that seems straight out of noir. Virginia Fisher saw firsthand how Irene was "tortured by demons from her past," especially the death of her beloved husband. That pain became unbearable during pre-production for *Postman*. Mayer knew Irene suffered from alcoholism (which would ultimately cause her to take her own life in 1962 when she leapt from an eleventh-floor window at Hollywood's Knickerbocker Hotel). Mayer grew concerned when the costume designer had been absent from the studio for more than a week. He dispatched MGM General Manager Eddie Mannix and Vice President Benny Thau—the studio's "fixers"—to check on her. They tracked down Irene in the midst of a drinking binge. Because of their close relationship, Mayer arrived at her house in Malibu with the script and a complete wardrobe breakdown in hand. He told her to "stay home and completely dry out," Fisher remembered, and he enlisted the studio's publicity department to concoct a cover story of a tonsillectomy. Studio drivers would take members of Irene's team to her beach house, and it was there they designed the costumes for *Postman*—all white with only two scenes dressing Lana in black.

Not a hint of this backstage drama appears in *The Postman Always Rings Twice*—the costume design and the clothes are quintessential Irene. She was a perfect designer for the 1940s, renowned for her form and fit, which was especially evident in her suiting. Cora's skirt suit reflects the impact of World War II rationing on style—the pencil skirt requiring a limited amount of fabric and a jacket that sports extra buttons for visual detail. The two-piece bathing suit that Lana wears along Laguna Beach is also significant in Irene's own design history. The bikini may have garnered international attention in 1946, but Irene had already designed one for Dolores del Río in *Flying Down to Rio*—the first time a two-piece bathing suit was ever seen on film. In *Postman* Turner makes a splash in a similar style that helped launch a trend, and its retro look often resurges in popularity.

Trend after trend can be traced back to the costumes in this film. The keyhole dresses Lana wears—in both black and white—became a signature style of the 1940s and so beloved that variations continue to appear in fashion collections. No costume, however, had as much impact as the one that introduces Cora to the audience. Cain's novel makes little of Cora's appearance and of Frank's reaction as he sees her for the first time: "Except for the shape, she wasn't any raving beauty, but she had a sulky look to her, and her lips stuck out in a way that made me want to mash them in for her."

In contrast, Garnett makes her entrance a cinematic moment, beginning as the camera spots a tube of lipstick rolling along the floor. The camera retraces its path and finds a pair of peep-toe pumps and lovely legs. Then Garnett and cinematographer Sidney Wagner, known for his work on *Cabin in the Sky* (1943), reveal Cora all at once as if she's an apparition—standing in the doorway in a white turban and sun suit. The color of the costume enhances the ethereal quality. Frank catches his breath at seeing her. Costumes carry a special significance when a character is introduced. They signal the character's personality, power (or lack thereof), and intentions. Cora's introduction packs a punch. At once, the audience knows she is both angel and devil. It is one of the great movie entrances of the 1940s and of film noir.

It's hard for Lana to seem innocent in this sexy swimsuit. Irene was the first to design a two-piece for film in *Flying Down to Rio*. (Everett Collection)

This all-black costume, one of only two in *Postman*, features another turban and keyhole dress. (Everett Collection)

Postman became an immediate and ongoing influence on fashion. Women in 1946 flocked to their department stores asking for all-white summer wardrobes. Today, white has become such a popular color that the "little white dress" is as much a wardrobe staple as its black counterpart. Even turbans have found a regular place on designer runways and in the closets of fashionistas.

Equally powerful was the film's impact on costume design. Kathleen Turner makes her own impressive screen entrance in white as femme fatale Matty Walker in the 1981 neo-noir *Body Heat*, with costume design by Renié. Director Brian De Palma, a student of cinema and fan of film noir, dressed leading ladies in white ensembles for both *Scarface* (1983), with costumes by Patricia Norris, and his neo-noir *Body Double* (1984), with Gloria Gresham as designer. Few can forget Sharon Stone's iconic moment in a white dress as seductress Catherine Tramell in the neo-noir *Basic Instinct*. Ellen Mirojnick designed that dress as well as Glenn Close's predominantly white wardrobe as the vengeful Alex Forrest in *Fatal Attraction* (1987).

Although many reasons led to the near all-white wardrobe in *Postman*, the vision for every costume was Irene's. Beginning with Lana's memorable entrance, the white (and sometimes black) wardrobe showcased Irene's well-known gift for form and fit, two attributes that never go out of fashion. Audiences might have been introduced to femme fatale Helen Grayle in a tantalizing white dress two years earlier in *Murder, My Sweet*—looking very much like Lana, in fact—but *The Postman Always Rings Twice* made the lasting impact on style.

Lana Turner looks luminous in this summery off-the-shoulder dress. (Greenbriar Collection)

Costume designer Edith Head was a master of minimalism, which can be seen in Ingrid Bergman's costumes in *Notorious*. (Everett Collection)

Notorious

Premiere: August 15, 1946
Director: Alfred Hitchcock
Costume designer: Edith Head
Studio: RKO

Alfred Hitchcock is almost a genre unto himself, perhaps best known for the thrillers he directed in the 1950s and 1960s. His partner during that period was Paramount's lead costume designer Edith Head. Together they created the image of the "Hitchcock Heroine," embodied by icy blondes like Grace Kelly in *Rear Window* (1954) and *To Catch a Thief* (1955), Doris Day in *The Man Who Knew Too Much* (1956), Kim Novak in *Vertigo* (1958), and Tippi Hedren in *The Birds* (1963).

Film fans debate whether to consider certain films from Hitchcock's career, even *Vertigo*, as film noir. Often included in the discussion is his black-and-white masterpiece, *Notorious*.

Many elements within *Notorious* align it with the film noir movement. Some of the genre's strongest cinematic influences are found in 1920s German Expressionism, and this inspiration is evident in the film. Hitchcock, however, was more than just inspired; he worked at Germany's UFA, the studio celebrated for productions like F. W. Murnau's *The Cabinet of Dr. Caligari* and Fritz Lang's *Metropolis*. While working with German filmmakers, Hitchcock learned what biographer Donald Spoto described as "the dynamics of the relationship between light and shadow," and it's beautifully realized in *Notorious* by cinematographer Ted Tetzlaff (*My Man Godfrey*).

Hitchcock's effective use of darkness adds to what Spoto called the "menacing, anxious, waiting quality, a quality of disequilibrium" throughout the picture, a prevalent mood in film noir. Adding to that mood is a screenplay from Ben Hecht, writer of the original gangster classic *Scarface*. He gave *Notorious* its tough edge and memorable dialogue such as, "Dry your eyes, baby. It's out of character." In the best of noir, there exists antagonism between the male and female leads. In *Notorious*, according to William Rothman writing for the Criterion Collection, the lead characters "make each other suffer and make themselves suffer" throughout their relationship.

Few suffer better on-screen than Ingrid Bergman, who plays the intrigante Alicia Huberman in *Notorious*. Like Grace Kelly, Bergman appeared in three Hitchcock films, but she had a slightly different relationship with the director than other Hitchcock heroines. Rather than let the director mold her into his fantasy girl, Ingrid served more as a collaborator and Hitchcock followed her lead in many ways.

The same could be said of producer David O. Selznick, who collaborated with Hitchcock and helped to preserve Bergman's innate style. In 1939 Bergman moved from Sweden to Hollywood after signing a four-year contract with Selznick. He enjoyed making stars of up-and-coming actresses. Vivien Leigh and Joan Fontaine had just soared to stardom with two Selznick productions that won Best Picture Oscars—*Gone With the Wind* followed by the Hitchcock-directed *Rebecca* (1940). David determined that Ingrid would be next.

In the beginning Selznick wanted to change many aspects of her appearance, from her eye-

Alfred Hitchcock's effective use of light and shadow adds to the menacing feel of this film noir. (GKB Collection)

brows to her teeth. Bergman immediately struck back and threatened to return to Sweden rather than change. Suddenly, Bergman's natural look became the basis of Selznick's approach in marketing her and her most celebrated quality. Selznick said to her, "I've got an idea that's so simple and yet no one in Hollywood has ever tried it before. Nothing about you is to be touched. Nothing altered. You remain yourself. You are going to be the first 'natural' actress."

It was a revolutionary idea in the midst of Hollywood's peak glamour years. "Everything had become very artificial and all hairdos," Bergman remembered. In contrast, "my hair got blown, my clothes were simple, I looked very simple and I acted like the girl next door." It was a very different style from that of stars like Lana Turner and Joan Crawford, women who enjoyed studio-provided wardrobes, hair, and makeup that made them look as exquisite off the screen as on it.

Selznick frequently loaned his actors to other studios and did so with Bergman. She made the most of every opportunity. Her first film under contract was a loan-out to Columbia in 1941 for *Adam Had Four Sons*. Perhaps her most famous loan-out came the next year in Warner

Bergman's natural style is on display in the film's sensual three-minute kissing scene. (Everett Collection)

Bros.' noir-adjacent *Casablanca*. She also made a splash at MGM in *Dr. Jekyll and Mr. Hyde* (1941) and *Gaslight* (1944), for which she won the Oscar for Best Actress. In between those productions, she was thrilled to learn that Ernest Hemingway had recommended her for the lead in the film version of his blockbuster novel *For Whom the Bell Tolls* (1943) at Paramount. Not only was it a part she wanted badly, but it's also where the actress would first meet and work with Edith Head.

Bergman found a natural ally in the costume designer. Head was already celebrated for her relative minimalism as well as her vocal support of rationing once World War II began. Bergman preferred simplicity in her style, and this approach proved helpful in her costumes. At nearly 5'10", Ingrid literally stood apart from other actresses. Other film noir stars tended to be on the petite side, such as Veronica Lake at 4'11", Gloria Swanson just hitting 5', and Barbara Stan-

Hitchcock and Head both worked around Bergman's height, including using the monochromatic design of the famous *Notorious* double v-neck gown. (Everett Collection)

wyck standing 5'3". Even many of the male stars, Bogart included, were shorter than Bergman. For this reason, she's often seen wearing flats or low heels in her movies, and this is true throughout *Notorious*. Fortunately, Head was well versed in using costume to address the challenges of height.

The idea for the film *Notorious* resulted from Selznick's encounter with a *Saturday Evening Post* short story called "The Song of the Dragon" about an actress who goes to bed with a spy to help with counterespionage. Hitchcock and writer Hecht adapted the story into one in which the U.S. government enlists the daughter of a convicted Nazi to infiltrate a group of German scientists living in Brazil. Selznick sold everything—director, script, and actors—to RKO for $800,000 and 50 percent of the profits. Because Bergman was now an in-demand star, she could name her own costume designer. She chose Edith Head.

Notorious would be the first of eleven films Head did with Hitchcock and the start of their legendary thirty-year relationship. Costumes were of utmost importance to Hitchcock; he was unusually detailed in his description of them even as the script was coming together. Head commented, "He was very specific about costumes for his leading ladies. He spoke a designer's language, even though he didn't know the first thing about clothes. He specified colors in the script if they were important. If he wanted a skirt that brushed a desk as a woman walked by, he spelled that out, too."

The picture began production just after the end of World War II, so the look, feel, and subject matter of *Notorious* are all in line with other noir of that period. But what sets it apart is the sophisticated, seductive style of Hitchcock. *Notorious* is the first Hitchcock film where costumes became a pronounced part of the style story. Style had always been important to Hitchcock, but the costumes were never as memorable prior to *Notorious*—ironic considering that the film was all about restraint.

Government agent T.R. Devlin (Cary Grant) is the very definition of restraint—all dispassion and self-control. The central love story between Devlin and Bergman's Alicia is built on hints of sadomasochism. He uses her love to push her into a mission as a "Mata Hari," and then his overwhelming jealousy makes him hate her for it. Neither can profess love for the other even though they obviously feel it in a most desperate way—similar to the relationship in *Gilda*.

The famous kissing scene in *Notorious* is an entire sequence dedicated to restraint. For nearly three minutes the actors skirted the Production Code by not locking lips for more than three seconds at a time. The heat between them creates a famously sensual moment in film. It should be no surprise, then, that the costumes carry through this theme.

To make Alicia believable as a spy, Hitchcock insisted that the costumes never become the focal point. This suited Bergman because she preferred a more subdued style. "Hers is elegance in the subtlest sense," said Head. "For a costume designer, an Ingrid Bergman picture is an education in restraint."

In key dramatic scenes, Alicia's costumes are restricted to black or white. The most memo-

The intense chemistry between Bergman and Cary Grant fuels the love-hate relationship in *Notorious*. (Everett Collection)

rable costume of the film is a black belted, long-sleeved gown with plunging necklines in both front and back. This Edith Head creation earns a sensational close-up. Hitchcock starts the scene with the camera at the top of the staircase. The view sweeps down the stairs and gradually closes in on Bergman's back in that gown. The acclaimed shot is a study in genius—and the gown is a study in simplicity. For subtle detail, Head adds slight ruching around the breasts, a design element she would explore further in her goddess gown designs for Grace Kelly in *To Catch a Thief*.

Bergman preferred minimal jewelry offscreen, and her character mirrors this by pairing only a few accessories with her black gown on-screen—diamond drop earrings, Alicia's wedding ring, and the all-important key to the wine cellar. In contrast, her all-white ensemble requires adornments to intensify its glamour. Head accents the simple round-neck jacket and flowing floor-length skirt with a white ermine wrap, long gloves, and a diamond necklace loaned to Alicia for the evening. Hitchcock and Head chose the color white to help the character project innocence during her first time spying at the mansion of former lover Alexander Sebastian (Claude Rains).

Before Alicia becomes a spy, however, the style story is very different. *Notorious* begins with

Alicia wears white to appear more innocent while spying for the first time at the Sebastian mansion. (GKB Collection)

the character as a playgirl, losing herself in alcohol and men to forget her father the traitor. The audience first sees Alicia as she hosts a cocktail party. Here she meets Devlin, and for this occasion Head put Bergman in another memorable costume—a short-sleeved, two-piece, sequined zebra-print dress. The print was strategic in a couple ways. Edith said, "The eye is immediately drawn to the stark contrast of black and white.... Visually, she became the most important woman in the room."

Costume designers use animal prints to say something significant about the character. In *Sunset Boulevard*, for instance, animal prints show the predatory nature of Norma Desmond. In *Notorious*, the look illustrates that the character is a promiscuous "drunk," a flaw in Alicia that the dialogue mentions time and again. The bare midriff reinforces that the character is a bit wild. The costume also sets up one of the film's sensual moments: Dev ties a scarf around Alicia's bare stomach so she doesn't catch cold. The move is sexual, but the costume avoided Breen office censorship by not revealing Bergman's décolletage or

Menswear was a part of 1940s style in addition to glamorous gowns. Bergman's costumes in *Notorious* include skirt suits and an equestrian ensemble. (Everett Collection)

belly button, which were considered too provocative. Alicia dons more formal attire, including smart skirt suits and an equestrian ensemble complete with necktie, later in the film when she's working as a spy.

Cary Grant's wardrobe in *Notorious* is as important as Bergman's. Grant served as an icon of men's style, and his Hitchcock films are particularly noteworthy. Head enjoyed dressing actors, though collaborating with Cary meant accepting that he would drive the design decisions. In the 1940s Grant often played characters with edge who treated women they claimed to care about less than nicely. *His Girl Friday* and *The Philadelphia Story* (1940) and *Suspicion* (1941) feature such characters. *Notorious* fit this mold and showed his evolving style from the "sack suits" of the 1930s to his single-vented suit of the 1940s to his classic double-vented look in 1950s films such as *North by Northwest* (1959). Double-vented jackets allowed the actor to put his hands in his pockets while standing—his signature pose—without wrinkling the fabric or exposing his derrière. His *Notorious* wardrobe included solid black suits, a black pin-striped suit, gray suits, and a tuxedo. This became something of a uniform for Grant, especially the tuxedo, which he wears in nearly all his films.

As with actresses, Grant had a few figure flaws, so all his suits on and off the screen were tailored for him and incorporated a number of tricks. His jackets were made broader and padded to address his thick neck and rounded narrow shoulders. To make him seem leaner, tailors cut the armholes a bit higher for him. Because Cary was particularly sensitive about his neck, he wore custom shirts that had higher-than-standard collars. For *Notorious* he fine-tuned his style, which included saying goodbye to hats—he wears only one and that briefly. It was an accessory he neither needed nor wanted.

"A hat to Cary Grant was just no damn good," said style expert Richard Torregrossa. Alfred Hitchcock appreciated all this attention to detail because, as his biographer Donald Spoto pointed out, no performance "would come closer to Hitchcock's self-understanding than—of all people—Cary Grant in *Notorious.*"

Hitchcock's later color motion pictures may be better remembered, but many filmmakers

In one of the noir's steamy moments, Dev ties a scarf around the bare midriff of Alicia's two-piece, sequined zebra-print dress. (Everett Collection)

and critics consider *Notorious* the fullest realization of his art. François Truffaut asserted, "In *Notorious* you have at once a maximum amount of stylization and a maximum of simplicity." This sums up the style of the costumes perfectly. Head's costume design delivers a master class in minimalism and serves as a reference point for Bergman's signature style.

As *New York Times* reporter Janet Maslin observed of Ingrid Bergman in a 1980 article about a *Notorious* screening at the Museum of Modern Art, "Perhaps she was more beautiful, more mysterious in *Casablanca*, but nowhere else than in *Notorious* was her naturalness more important on the screen."

Although Head designed Bergman's wardrobe to convey restraint, two costumes still stand out and are influential in fashion: the black, double-plunging V-neck gown and the two-piece, sequined zebra-print dress. Both remain fixtures in fashion design along with the overall style of the film.

Head's double-plunging yet subtle V-neck gown has remained influential in fashion. (Everett Collection)

Humphrey Bogart and Lauren Bacall embody film noir style in *The Big Sleep*. (Everett Collection)

The Big Sleep

Premiere: August 23, 1946
Director: Howard Hawks
Costume designer: Leah Rhodes
Studio: Warner Bros.

Beginning with Humphrey Bogart and Lauren Bacall smoking cigarettes in silhouette against the opening credits, *The Big Sleep* looks like the essence of film noir. Author Raymond Chandler and director Howard Hawks gave it all the darkness and danger that is the genre's trademark: pornography, extortion, blackmail, adultery, and murder. And then there are the dames. So many dames. A young nympho socialite. A protective older sister. A greedy grifter. A sexy bookshop owner. A sassy cab driver. A gangster's wife. The film's famously incomprehensible plot is superseded by a great cast of characters and a string of engaging scenes that dramatically dissolve from one to the next.

Bogart plays private eye Philip Marlowe and spends much of his time in a trench coat searching for clues in the pouring rain in Los Angeles. As Vivian Rutledge, the daughter of Marlowe's wealthy client, Bacall furthers "The Look" she established in *To Have and Have Not*. *The Big Sleep* is the film that solidifies the style of both Bogart and Bacall.

The screenplay for *The Big Sleep* was based on the book of the same name by Chandler. He was the master of what author and film noir authority David Hogan called "the dark playground of wartime and postwar Los Angeles." *The Big Sleep* features Chandler's favorite detective working his way through the corruption of the dark city as he falls for a woman who may or may not be a femme fatale.

In many ways *The Big Sleep* is a follow up to *To Have and Have Not* due to the cast and crew who worked on both productions. Hawks directed both and brought back Jules Furthman and William Faulkner to write the screenplay, although much of the dialogue benefited from the inclusion of Leigh Brackett. Brackett was a first-time novelist with a "tough, hard-boiled prose style" that impressed Hawks, according to his biographer Todd McCarthy—and intrigued him even more when he discovered that Leigh was a woman.

The banter in *The Big Sleep* is classic noir with lines such as, "You know, you're the second guy I've met today that seems to think a gat in the hand means the world by the tail." An uncredited assist on the script came from *Casablanca* screenwriter Philip Epstein, who came up with additional scenes between Bogart and Bacall after *To Have and Have Not* proved them to be a popular on-screen couple. Epstein's major contribution was a discussion of horse racing over drinks that had nothing to do with equestrians and everything to do with sex.

Sexual attraction was an important aspect of Hawks' films, especially so in *The Big Sleep*. "In line with Hawks' vision of an ideal world, every woman in [the movie] makes a pass at Bogart," said McCarthy. The women are just as insolent as the men and every argument masks an attempt at seduction. Because the Production Code was in effect, the writers carefully crafted the dialogue to stymie any censorship from Joseph Breen.

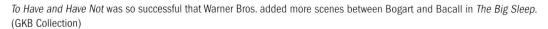

To Have and Have Not was so successful that Warner Bros. added more scenes between Bogart and Bacall in *The Big Sleep*. (GKB Collection)

A strong but sexy metallic jacket accompanies a discussion of horse racing that has nothing to do with equestrians and everything to do with sex. (Everett Collection)

The innuendo-laced dialogue and clever comebacks only begin to define the style of *The Big Sleep*. Sid Hickox's cinematography is good in *To Have and Have Not* and great in *The Big Sleep*. His dreamy lighting is on display from the start with those smoky opening credits. The "characters are suffused with a glow that fades into shadow ... [and] sometimes the faces look like pieces of Renaissance art," noted David Hogan. Bacall has one of the great faces in film, an actress who made the most of her success after being discovered on the cover of *Harper's Bazaar*.

Lauren became a temptress who seduced both Bogart and the audience with the intensity of her eyes. She was so known for those eyes that "The Look" became part of a strong publicity push from Warner Bros. for *The Big Sleep*. *TIME* magazine famously pronounced: "Lauren Bacall has cinema personality to burn.... She has a javelin-like vitality, a born dancer's eloquence in movement, a fierce female shrewdness and a special sweet-sourness. With these faculties plus a stone-crushing self-confidence and a trombone voice ... she does a wickedly good job of sizing up male prospects."

Much of her attitude and her character's costumes came courtesy of the mentoring of Howard and Slim Hawks. A socialite and successful model, Slim was long celebrated for her style and always included on fashion "best dressed" lists. Her husband also loved her strong, assertive personality, so he had both writers and costume designers take their cues from Slim for Bacall's characters in *To Have and Have Not* and *The Big Sleep*.

Milo Anderson designed Bacall's costumes in *To Have and Have Not*. For *The Big Sleep* and later *Key Largo*, Bacall worked with Leah Rhodes. Rhodes began in a modest role at Warner Bros. as a buyer for designers. She worked her way up to assisting head costume designer Orry-Kelly, eventually taking over his duties in 1942 when he enlisted in the Army. She would more than prove her talent with an Oscar win for costume design of Errol Flynn's *Adventures of Don Juan* (1948).

Rhodes excelled on tough-guy pictures and infused them with style. Besides her experience with Bogart and Bacall, she would also design for the gangster classic *White Heat* (1949) and for Alfred Hitchcock's noir-adjacent *Strangers on a Train* (1951).

The trio of Rhodes, Anderson, and Orry-Kelly were instrumental in establishing the style of the Warner Bros. studio as well as for both Bogart and Bacall. Taking inspiration from Slim Hawks, Rhodes designed the suiting that became identified with *The Big Sleep*. The houndstooth suit Bacall wears is almost an exact copy of one of Slim's own, right down to the black round-neck top underneath the jacket. The beret from *To Have and Have Not* makes a reappearance with the ensemble. The houndstooth suit has remained influential in fashion with versions frequently coming down runways and appearing in magazine editorials.

Suits with pencil skirts were at their height of popularity during the war years due to the economy of fabric, and this helped Bacall's on-screen style resonate with audiences. She loved the look offscreen as well, wearing a pale pink wool suit—not beige, which is often reported—to marry Bogart after *The Big Sleep*. Her costumes in the film include sensible but stylish belted dresses, another staple in Bacall's own wardrobe. And, as a sign of the times and asserting her own

The battling bookstore managers are very different women with very different styles. (Both photos, Everett Collection)

style, she opens the movie wearing pants.

The costumes for Carmen Sternwood—former model Martha Vickers—are very different from Vivian's. Carmen is "a lewd, lascivious child ever on the lookout for mischief to stir up, [who] encouraged thoughts of boundless depravity," and her clothes reflect this right from the start. Marlowe meets Carmen in the foyer of the Sternwood mansion, and she's all legs in white shorts with black polka dots. Polka dots were a popular pattern of the 1940s, and Carmen wears them to appear more innocent than she really is.

When Carmen breaks into Marlowe's apartment, she waits for him in a polka dot dress so snug it proves she's anything but a child. (In the novel she waits for him stark naked in his bed.) Carmen is clearly a troublemaker, and her costumes reflect her dramatic ways, such as suits paired with silk hoods. She wears one when she goes to Joe Brody's apartment to reclaim a risqué photo. In the novel she's naked in the picture, but for the film she wore an Asian-inspired sleeveless silk top and skirt. That exotic flair can be seen in the production design as well, particularly anything associated with the extortionist Arthur Gwynn Geiger.

There's more style of note in *The Big Sleep* thanks to its battling bookstore managers. On the dark side of the street is Geiger's accomplice, Agnes (Sonia Darrin). Agnes presents herself like an art gallery curator adorned in high fashion. There's an edge to

Carmen's style leans toward the dramatic, including the exotic Asian-inspired sleeveless silk top and skirt she wears to pose for pornographic photos. (Top photo, GKB Collection; bottom photo, Everett Collection)

Above: Bacall's houndstooth suit continues to be influential on fashion. Below: Warner Bros. costume designer Leah Rhodes was behind the Bogart-Bacall style in *The Big Sleep* and *Key Largo*. (Both photos, Everett Collection)

her, enhanced by her amoral character, that is reflected in her style choices. She meets Marlowe for the first time in a black dress with tiered ruffles accessorized with a dramatic brooch, belt, and loads of jewelry. On another occasion, she's in an exotic silk wrap blouse fastened around a dark high-waisted skirt with another brilliant brooch. In contrast, the Acme Bookstore seller across the street, played by a young Dorothy Malone, is down-to-earth, knowledgeable, and a real "pal" to Marlowe. Polka dots make another appearance in her tie-neck dress, which has a sleeveless dress layered over it and belted. The scene in the bookshop is memorable, not only for the undeniable chemistry between the actors, but also because it's a classic—studious girl takes off her glasses, literally lets down her hair, and transforms into the sexiest woman on earth right before the audience's eyes.

Although each of the female characters is a scene-stealer and exudes a certain strength seen in women during the war, *The Big Sleep* is best known for classic Bogart style. His look builds on the work of Orry-Kelly in *The Maltese Falcon* and *Casablanca*. Marlowe's double-breasted khaki trench coat and dark felt, snap-brim Royal Stetson fedora are the essentials of his wardrobe. They became essentials for other noir heroes as well, such as Dick Powell, Alan Ladd, and Robert Mitchum. This look is distinctly of the era because trench coats were a part of the military uniform that often was repurposed in civilian life. This reuse was particularly true of soldiers who struggled on their return after the war. In fact, Marlowe is called "soldier" by bad guy Eddie Mars. Underneath the trench Marlowe wears his own unique uniform, composed of an uncomplicated birds-eye wool suit with a single-breasted, two-button jacket. He has a handkerchief at the ready and keeps his keys on a chain attached to his belt loop. And despite mocking others for waving guns around, Marlowe makes sure he has access to one, including a revolver hidden in a secret panel in his car.

Marlowe dresses up from time to time, favoring a dark double-breasted pin-striped suit when going out, such as when he visits Eddie Mars at the casino or meets Vivian for drinks. He also has alternate outerwear in the form of a glen-plaid topcoat, which he wears to visit a police crime scene late at night. Every aspect of the character and his wardrobe fits Bogart perfectly. Biographer Stefan Kanfer agreed: "Humphrey gave his Marlowe the essential tone of film noir. He seemed born to play this part, with a face as stark and angular as the cinematography." Marlowe's look was largely the collaboration between Warner Bros. costume designers and Bogart, with some guidance from Chandler's novel (and those of Dashiell Hammett before him). There was an authenticity to Bogart and the parts he played. Said Roger Ebert in his review of *The Big Sleep*, "Bogart himself made personal style into an art form."

Much of the wardrobes of the women in *The Big Sleep* is timeless, however, the biggest style story still comes from Bogart. His costumes came straight from his own closet, and his trench coat in particular befits a genre in which not everyone lives happily ever after. Over the years trench coats have grown in popularity and become a staple with women as well, led by fashion houses like Burberry, which made the originals during World Wars I and II. London clothier Aquascutum even makes a trench named after Bogart and fashioned after the one he wears in *The Big Sleep*. The style in this 1946 noir has transcended film. With it, Bogart and Bacall have become part of American culture.

The gown in *The Big Sleep* is less glamorous than others of the era, which reflects Bacall's personal style. (Everett Collection)

Ava Gardner as femme fatale Kitty Collins in the signature, one-shouldered black satin gown of *The Killers*. (Everett Collection)

The Killers

Premiere: August 28, 1946
Director: Robert Siodmak
Costume designer: Vera West
Studio: Universal

Right woman. Right role. Right dress. These three ingredients make Robert Siodmak's *The Killers* so memorable—a film noir that created a star in Ava Gardner as femme fatale Kitty Collins and featured costume design that made an impact on fashion the moment the picture premiered.

The whole movie projects style, largely because of the stunning cinematography of Woody Bredell that starts with the shadowy silhouettes of two gunmen stalking toward a small-town diner. The opening scenes of the killers hunting Pete Lund—Burt Lancaster in his film debut—came from Ernest Hemingway's 1927 short story of the same name. The rest of the story, told in flashback, was created by screenwriter Anthony Veiller with uncredited contributions from John Huston and Richard Brooks, who later scripted *Deadline—U.S.A.* (1952).

A major component of the innovative style is the film's costume design, which includes a black satin gown that became the picture's signature. There are several stories behind the wardrobe, which reflects the end of the war years with its inclusion of accessible separates along with aspirational glamour. All the stories involve gifted costume designer Vera West, who had a life—and death—to rival any plot line in film noir.

On June 29, 1947, only months after she retired from her near two-decade tenure at Universal and started a couturier at the Beverly-Wilshire Hotel, West was found floating face down in her pool. The medical examiner ruled the death a suicide with not one but two bizarre notes left behind. Each claimed she had been blackmailed for years, although neither explained why.

"This is the only way," one stated, "I am tired of being blackmailed."

A second note written on the back of a torn greeting card stated, "The fortune-teller told me there was only one way to duck the blackmail I've paid for 23 years. Death."

The story and suicide seemed suspicious, especially since her death coincided with an argument Vera had with her husband, who had no real alibi the night of the crime.

This level of intrigue makes it surprising that West has remained one of the lesser-known costume designers from Hollywood's Golden Age. She started designing in her youth and worked as a dressmaker both before and after attending the Philadelphia School of Design for Women, now the Moore College of Art & Design. There she studied under Lucy Christiana, Lady Duff-Gordon, who ran the influential international couturier Lucile. In 1926 Vera headed west to Los Angeles and after only two years found herself head of costume design at Universal Pictures. She remained at the studio until 1947, engaging in a career in film that lasted longer than those of legendary contemporaries Adrian at MGM and Travis Banton at Paramount.

In contrast to the fashion-forward films that both MGM and Paramount were known for, Universal focused more on monster movies like *Dracula* and *Frankenstein*. They would become classics in their own right, casting West as the queen of horror couture. She wove elegance into her designs. For example, Elsa Lanchester never looked more striking than in *The Bride of Frankenstein*. In the next decade Universal would become known for noir, and *The Killers* would finally give Vera the opportunity to make her mark on fashion history.

Others besides West claimed this film noir a career turning point. Ava Gardner had been working at MGM since 1941, but it was the loan to Universal for *The Killers* that gave the actress a breakthrough part. Metro had signed Gardner to a contract for her obvious beauty. Her career began when one of their legal runners saw her portrait in a New York photography studio. A subsequent screen test caused director Al Altman to send a telegram to Louis B. Mayer stating, "She can't sing, she can't act, she can't talk. She's terrific!" She couldn't act, but she was absolutely stunning on and off the screen—dark hair, emerald eyes, ivory skin. Every man fell in love the moment he looked at her.

Costume designer Vera West with Hugh Herbert on the set of *La Conga Nights* (1940). (Everett Collection)

Kitty is capable of seducing poor Pete Lund—and every other man—even in a simple cotton blouse and skirt. (Everett Collection)

MGM invested in the starlet straight away, starting with acting lessons and vocal training to erase a strong North Carolina accent. Yet year after year the studio neglected to put her in substantive roles that capitalized on all Ava had to offer. She got only the smallest of parts, mostly uncredited; Gardner had no film credit for her first fifteen roles at MGM. Instead, she spent much of her time in bathing suits on the beach modeling for publicity photos. Then began the pattern of other studios borrowing Ava for their own productions—first, Monogram Pictures for *Ghosts on the Loose* (1943), then United Artists for *Whistle Stop* (1946), and then Universal. It was her performance in *Whistle Stop* that inspired producer Mark Hellinger to hire her. Not only was she stunning, but he believed she had the ability to play more than a sexpot and could tap into emotions simmering beneath the surface. Hellinger was confident that "Ava Gardner could convince audiences a man would steal, go to prison, [and] die for her." Even though MGM had no projects for her at the time, they still made Hellinger pay to borrow the twenty-three-year-old siren from the studio. For all these reasons, the role of Kitty Collins seems like Gardner's film debut. It's certainly the picture that turned her into a star.

The Killers made Gardner the object of every man's desire. Although she has less screen time than her co-stars, her character is the dark heart of the movie. Much of it centers on her, beginning with the film's extraordinary chiaroscuro lighting, creating dramatic contrast. Director

The lethal "sweater girl" lounges in bed at the poker game where the caper begins. (Everett Collection)

Robert Siodmak had started his career at Germany's UFA, the studio that gave birth to German Expressionism and helped inspire the look of film noir.

For *The Killers*, Hellinger asked Siodmak and Bredell to light scenes "exactly as they would be seen in real life." This meant using far fewer lights than were common in Hollywood productions and translated to actors needing less makeup. In fact, Ava was largely bare-faced through the movie. Bredell recalled, "All we did was rub a little Vaseline into her skin for a sheen effect." Her natural complexion was such a pure white that Bredell based his lighting around it. Their approach would be realism, from the lighting to her looks.

Writer James Agee described the style of *The Killers* as "jazzed-up realism" and that included the costumes too. For all the glamour manifested through the genre of film noir, especially those pictures celebrated for their style, *The Killers* stands out for featuring the kind of clothes that average women wore during the 1940s. For example, in two scenes Gardner wears a modest skirt and cotton blouse—a checked pattern in one scene and a solid in another. Yet the simplicity of these ensembles does nothing to diminish what Gardner biographer Lee Server describes as Kitty's "haunting erotic presence" in those moments, including one where she passionately kisses Pete Lund. Gardner's sex appeal is proven further at a poker game where the caper begins. West shows just how sexy simple can be by dressing Ava in a sweater and skirt, shoes off, watching the group steely-eyed while seductively sprawled across a bed.

West gives the audience many clues to Kitty's character through costume. In a scene toward the end of the movie, she wears a trench coat to meet Reardon (Edmond O'Brien) at a café. Film noir is filled with leading men wearing trench coats—it's a signature style. It communicates something significant, then, when the femme fatale adopts a look that's generally reserved for men. She's the one who's really in charge, at the center of a double cross, and determined to get away with it all. In that coat, O'Brien remembered, Gardner "gave a convincing account of a deceiving woman about to be caught."

Garbo first wore a trench coat in 1928's *A Woman of Affairs*, but in *The Killers* Ava took the style further in mainstream fashion. The look would also influence future costume design—the trench would appear on other style mavens such as Marlene Dietrich in *A Foreign Affair* (1948), with costume design by Edith Head, and Audrey Hepburn in both *Breakfast at Tiffany's* (1961) and *Charade* (1963), both designed by Hubert de Givenchy. Beyond film, television costume designer Lyn Paolo used the trench to convey Olivia Pope's covert life as a political fixer in the television series *Scandal* (2013). It's a trend in fashion that can be traced back to *The Killers*; Ava Gardner helped the trench evolve into something timeless in a woman's wardrobe.

Ava Gardner's Kitty is a heartless black widow who betrays anyone in the way of her getting what she wants, which West communicates through her costume design. Even the stolen jewelry Kitty wears—a brooch pinned to a dress with a classic 1940s sweetheart neckline—looks like a spider. Kitty exudes trouble the moment she is introduced, sitting at a piano with her back to the camera, a single strap of her dress cutting between her shoulder blades. When she stands, she pauses to model the gown in its entirety; black satin with a strap starting at the center of

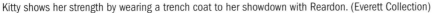

Kitty shows her strength by wearing a trench coat to her showdown with Reardon. (Everett Collection)

Even the stolen jewelry Kitty wears—a brooch pinned to a dress with a classic 1940s sweetheart neckline—tells the audience she is a heartless black widow. (GKB Collection)

her décolletage and crossing over her left shoulder. It's an aspect of the design that may have been prompted by the Production Code since censors warned the production: "Care will be needed with this low-cut gown."

West makes the most of the fabric, pinching and draping it in ways that would catch the light and make the "phosphorescent material [give] off subtle glints in strategic places," according to one columnist. Fellow Universal costume designer Yvonne Wood recalled Vera's vision of the character's backstory in her most famous design: "It looked expensive; it was expensive; but it just missed enough so it was slightly lacking in good taste. It was the type of gown a girl of that background buys when she suddenly has a lot of money."

This level of detail helps Ava's passionate portrayal of Kitty Collins stand out among what Gardner biographer Lee Server described as a "sisterhood of memorable femmes fatales, duplicitous dames, and lethal spider women." Gardner personified the devil in a black dress.

The Killers proved a huge hit with the public in 1946 and also earned critical acclaim, receiving Academy Award nominations for direction, screenplay, and score. What's far too often overlooked is the powerful contribution of its costume design. Images of Gardner in the black one-shouldered gown appeared in posters as part of the publicity campaign that had people lining up around the block. The one-strap design continues to influence style on the red carpet, from the SAG Awards to the Golden Globes. It's so well known that its architecture can be seen even in swimsuits.

Ava Gardner shot to popularity in movie magazines and won a *Look* magazine award as Hollywood's most promising newcomer. She was the perfect actress to play femme fatale Kitty Collins, and Vera West's wardrobe for her—the black satin gown in particular—the perfect attire to make film and fashion history.

Vera West's sexy one-shouldered satin gown for *The Killers* secured a place in both fashion and film history. (Everett Collection)

The Post-War Years
1947—1950

Christian Dior's "New Look" shown in all its glory in a voluminous evening gown. (Alamy Collection)

Boom, Blacklist, and a New Look

In many ways, Charles Dickens' "best of times" and "worst of times" opening to *A Tale of Two Cities* could have been describing the post-war years in America. The country was in the middle of an economic boom that would stretch into the 1950s, a boom fueled by the many benefits of the Servicemen's Readjustment Act of 1944, better known as the G.I. Bill. This piece of legislation "provided liberal unemployment benefits, gave veterans preference in finding jobs, offered them substantial educational assistance (in the form of tuition payments and supplementary grants to meet living expenses), and guaranteed loans for the purchase of a small business, farm, or home," wrote Allan Winkler in *Home Front U.S.A.* In 1947 alone, veterans accounted for 49 percent of college admissions. And by the time the bill expired in 1952, the government had backed nearly 2.4 million home loans.

The country's overall unemployment would average only 4.6 percent between 1947 and 1950, which translated to tremendous prosperity in peacetime. For these reasons and for the optimism that came from so many opportunities, the post-war era would be remembered as America's golden age. Yet, something very dark emerged in America alongside all the light.

During World War II Americans had bravely fought for freedom abroad. Ironically, freedom was facing a challenge at home on the heels of the Allied victory. With the onset of the Cold War, the country became consumed by a paranoia about Communism. Many people were persecuted and prosecuted because of it, mostly through the House Un-American Activities Committee (HUAC) created in 1938. By the end of 1946, HUAC was a major political force and it took mere months for the committee to target Hollywood and tear it apart. In May 1947 HUAC chairman J. Parnell Thomas announced, "Hundreds of very prominent film capital people have been named as Communists to us." In fact, there was little Communist influence in the movies and nothing to suggest there was any intention to take over Hollywood, but the committee began hearings to make Thomas' statement seem true.

Many Hollywood conservatives emerged as vehement anti-Communists and became friendly witnesses for the committee. They included studio heads Jack L. Warner and Louis B. Mayer as well as actors Robert Taylor and Robert Montgomery, who would make *Lady in the Lake* during this period.

Many others in Hollywood expressed outrage at what they saw as a gross violation of the First Amendment. John Huston, Humphrey Bogart, and Lauren Bacall traveled to Washington, D.C., with others to passionately protest the hearings. It wasn't enough. Edward Dmytryk, who had directed *Murder, My Sweet*, was among a group of writers, directors, and a producer who refused to cooperate. The Hollywood Ten, as they were called, were charged with contempt of Congress and thrown in jail. The unjustified inquisition went on for years, and the consequences were high. People lost their careers, lost their friends, and even lost their lives as a result. The suffering and alienation helped fuel the film noir from this time, but the hearings and resulting blacklist have remained a scar on a nation that considers itself the land of the free and prides itself on civil rights.

In the midst of such ugliness, it was fashion that offered a distraction and boosted America's morale. For years, fashion had been restricted in a number of ways. Every resource had been prioritized to the war effort, and rationing existed from March 1942 to October 1946. With Limitation Order 85, the War Production Board controlled the type and amount of material used in women's clothing; the order might have dictated more austere design for the war years, but Hollywood showed women they could still be stylish. Costume designers set trends all over the world and some of their success stemmed from their ability to predict those trends.

In 1946 fashion journalist Bettina Bedwell said: "One thing a designer in charge of one of the giant Hollywood

Nine of The Hollywood Ten (left to right): Adrian Scott, Edward Dmytryk, Samuel Ornitz, Lester Cole, Herbert Biberman, Albert Maltz, Alvah Bessie, John Lawson, and Ring Lardner, Jr. Not pictured: Dalton Trumbo. (Everett Collection)

One month before the Hollywood Blacklist was established, life-long Republican Gary Cooper appeared as a friendly witness for the House Un-American Activities Committee. (Everett Collection)

movie studio wardrobe departments has to be is a good prophet. Pictures are dressed a long time ahead, sometimes several years, and when the clothes are seen by you and me, they have to be in style. If they produce snickers, the designer's career is over—but really over." Bedwell's comment comes close to describing the reality of 1947 when a seismic shift in fashion took costume designers by surprise and leveled many Hollywood productions.

Paris had lost its place as the center of fashion when the German occupation began in June 1940. After the war the couturiers reclaimed their international customers and returned to launching their new lines each spring and fall. On February 12, 1947, then-unknown designer Christian Dior presented his *La Corelle* collection, so called because of "the way the skirts fanned out like petals from a stem-like waist," according to columnist Annalisa Barbieri. It was the look of the Belle Époque complete with corsets, multiple layers, and many mechanisms to enhance the hips and breasts. Voluminous skirts used twenty yards of the most luxurious fabric and were finished with elaborate beading and embroidery.

"I designed clothes for flowerlike women," Dior said, "with rounded shoulders, full feminine busts and hand-span waists above enormous spreading skirts." Nothing could have been further from the austere fashions of the war years. Dior redefined the silhouette and put style on the path to the 1950s. Representatives of American fashion magazines traveled to Paris to cover the collections and sat in shock in Dior's salon. *Harper's Bazaar*'s visionary editor-in-chief Carmel Snow had been an early advocate of many talented designers such as Cristobel Balenciaga and Hubert de Givenchy. She now said to Dior, "It's quite a revolution, dear Christian. Your dresses have such a new look." From this point on, the Corelle collection would be known as the New Look.

Dior's creations were so new that many considered them unpatriotic, and the collection inspired a violent reaction. "In Britain, France, and the U.S., outraged women even attacked the earliest wearers of the New Look on the street, incensed at what they saw as a waste of material," reported *The Guardian's* Linda Grant. England was still suffering from the austerity of the war. Corsets, for example, continued to be banned because of that country's ongoing rationing. America had lifted its own rationing program only months earlier, so groups like the "Little Below the Knee Club" staged protests in Chicago and elsewhere. Even Parisians took offense at the extravagance of the New Look. French designer Coco Chanel, who had made her name by moving women away from the corset, was among the protesting voices.

Fashion designer Christian Dior fitting one of his couture gowns to perfection. (Alamy Collection)

As late as autumn 1948 photographer Walter Carone captured a dark moment on the Rue Lepic. He witnessed women who were outraged by the waste of fabric tearing a New Look dress off a young woman. "It is difficult to overstate the impact of the New Look," said fashion historian David Bond. "It would have been considered an extravagant fashion [even] in affluent times."

Dior's collection proved a painful lesson for Hollywood. At first, costume designers tried to ignore the New Look, believing that no one in America would be interested. By July 1947, however, the writing was on the wall. The New Look had quickly moved past a trend and redefined the fashion of the era, making Hollywood productions suddenly seem out of date. That month reporter Carol Adams wrote, "In a little while, modern pictures that are one year old will look like period films. That's how great the changes are."

Paramount's costume designer Edith Head recognized the enormity of the industry's mistake. "I learned my lesson the hard way," she admitted. "Just after Dior brought out the New Look, every film that I had done in the past few months looked like something from the bread lines."

It was a crisis that demanded immediate action. Costumes had to be altered or remade entirely. At Paramount alone, the alterations for extras included 600 evening dresses, 400 day dresses, and 450 suits. Dior, however, didn't just have an effect on pictures in production. Edith Head biographer Paddy Calistro said, "Every movie that was made in 1946 and held on the shelf until 1947 looked miserably dated from a fashion point of view." The problem proved so prevalent and so significant that some films were just scrapped. The only silver lining was that the lesson had indeed been learned. "It took the New Look to teach me that moderation is important in the motion picture business," Head concluded.

The streamlined style of the war years had fit film noir incredibly well. As a result, the costumes in pictures such as *Dead Reckoning, Lady in the Lake*, and *Out of the Past* (all 1947) as

Edith Head makes some alterations to Lizabeth Scott's costumes for *Desert Fury* (1947). (Everett Collection)

well as in *The Lady from Shanghai* (1948) didn't look out of date, nor did they suffer as others did. There would be a slow softening of the silhouette in the genre through the end of the 1940s.

Fashion columnist Eileen Callahan reported on the subtle changes that started to appear in the movies: "Even the classic tailored suit has been softened. Its sharp, padded shoulders now have a more natural, rounded line. The jacket waistline is seamed more definitely so that the waist looks smaller. The hip area is extended slightly. Lapels are rounded rather than pointed. Pockets and cuffs are prettied with stitching. Buttons are decorative. Edgings are scalloped. The straight line has given way to the curve."

Callahan cites Rita Hayworth's black wool suit with satin trim in *The Lady from Shanghai* as an example of where the softening can be seen. Gloria Swanson's costumes in *Sunset Boulevard* show a style that mixes the Silent Era with the New Look, which perfectly personifies the character of Norma Desmond.

The New Look actually added to the alienation felt in the late 1940s. Although many women were eager to indulge in every aspect of femininity after years of deprivation, the style corresponded to societal change that wasn't welcome to everyone. Most women who had joined the workforce during World War II wanted to continue working, but the influx of men from the military forced them to return to being homemakers after the war. Their new life now had a uniform and even an attitude thanks to the New Look. Dior said of his collection, "I brought back the art of pleasing."

This dramatic swing from independence to suggested subservience was something of a shock to women. In the 1940s they had finally found themselves on near-equal footing with men in the workforce. Fashion had reflected this, especially in the suiting. Styles in the 1920s and 1930s had intended to liberate women from the artificial constraints imposed by corsets, yet women found themselves all the way back at the turn of the century in more ways than one. Fortunately, film noir was a place where women could still be strong and go toe-to-toe with men.

In this post-war time of upheaval, one change was for the better. In 1948 the Academy of Motion Picture Arts and Sciences created an award for costume design; there had been nothing to acknowledge the art form for the first twenty-one years of the Academy. The award was originally divided into two categories, one for color films and one for black and white, which would merge into one award in 1967. That means only four of the films noir presented in this book were even eligible for this Oscar: *The Lady from Shanghai*, *Out of the Past*, *The Asphalt Jungle*, and *Sunset Boulevard*. None were nominated. This delay in recognizing the contributions of costume designers is an injustice to the vast number of talented artists who were ignored. MGM's legendary costume designer Adrian, for instance, retired from Hollywood in 1942, but at least the world can see the greatness of his costumes from films such as *Dinner at Eight* (1933) and *The Women* (1939) in their ongoing impact on fashion.

The New Look may have turned attention to Paris again as a trendsetter, but the massive influence of Hollywood was far from over. Many of the costume designers from 1940s noir would go on to create some of the most famous looks in 1950s film and television. For Edith Head, the decade would be her most prolific period, ultimately resulting in eight Oscars for costume design that included *All About Eve* (1950), *A Place in the Sun* (1951), and *Roman Holiday* (1953). She would also be celebrated for creating the look of Alfred Hitchcock's heroines, from Grace Kelly in *Rear Window* to Kim Novak in the color noir *Vertigo*. Jean Louis would continue working on Columbia noir and design for bad girl Gloria Grahame in *The Big Heat* and *Human Desire*. Once he moved on to Universal, he would be known for his work with style stars Doris Day in *Pillow Talk* and Lana Turner in *Imitation of Life*. MGM's Helen Rose also designed for Turner, winning an Oscar for her costumes in *The Bad and the Beautiful* (1952) as well as another Oscar for Susan

Hayward's costumes in *I'll Cry Tomorrow* (1955). It could be argued that Edward Stevenson was the most influential costume designer of the decade. His shirtwaist dresses for longtime friend Lucille Ball in her TV series *I Love Lucy* followed Dior's lead and shaped much of 1950s style for mainstream America.

European couture might have come roaring back in the late 1940s, but its influence would continue to be checked and challenged. Hollywood costume designers, including those who created the look of 1940s film noir, would still be the source of style inspiration around the world for decades to come.

Edith Head would incorporate elements of the New Look into Grace Kelly's celebrated opening costume in *Rear Window*. (Everett Collection)

The *Dead Reckoning* costume that seduced audiences into theater seats: a black halter gown with a plunging neckline in both front and back. (Everett Collection)

Dead Reckoning

Premiere: January 2, 1947
Director: John Cromwell
Costume designer: Jean Louis
Studio: Columbia

Dead Reckoning might not be among the most memorable movies in the dark world of noir, but a number of things make it worth watching. Humphrey Bogart plays Capt. Warren "Rip" Murdock, a paratrooper who is flown from Paris to Washington, D.C., in order to receive the Distinguished Service Cross. His best friend Sgt. Johnny Drake (William Prince) is to be awarded the Medal of Honor, but he suddenly takes a powder when he realizes his true identity will be revealed.

From that point on, many mysteries unfold for Murdock to solve, starting with a murder that has entangled sultry blonde siren Coral Chandler—Lizabeth Scott in her first portrayal of a femme fatale. Her style is a big reason to dive into *Dead Reckoning*. Columbia's head couturier, Jean Louis, referenced other films noir in Scott's costumes, but he also gave her a look very much her own.

Film noir had World War II in its soul. Stories emerged from soldiers returning from the war and struggling to find their place in the world. Most often the references to the war were subtle. In *The Big Sleep*, for example, gangster Eddie Mars refers to private eye Philip Marlowe as "soldier." *Dead Reckoning* is different; references to the war are direct, and it's central to the overall story. Five veterans who experienced the horrors of war, all of whom earned Purple Hearts, were behind the story and screenplay.

At the start of *Dead Reckoning*, Rip and Johnny are being whisked back to America after active duty, and the audience can immediately sense their commitment to one another. When his best friend disappears, Murdock embarks on a mission filled with military expressions like "breaking camp," "clear of the beachhead," and "Geronimo." Even the film's title "dead reckon-

Dead Reckoning is a true post-war film noir; veterans are at the center of its story. (Everett Collection)

ing" has its origins in navigation.

Screenwriter Steve Fisher knew the world of noir in addition to his experience with the war. He had been responsible for both the novel and screenplay for *I Wake Up Screaming* as well as an adaptation of Raymond Chandler's *Lady in the Lake*. *Dead Reckoning* alludes to several film noir predecessors. From *Gilda* comes the dangerous nightclub with "Amado Mío" playing in the background. *The Big Sleep* inspires the scene of an intrigante gambling thousands at the order of a gangster club owner. And from *The Maltese Falcon* the picture gets Bogart suffering from a doped drink as well as memorable dialogue near its conclusion:

Rip: "You're going to fry, Dusty."

Coral: "Rip, can't we put this behind us? Can't you forget?"

Rip: "I can't forget I might die tomorrow. Suppose you're sore at me some morning for something? Then there's Johnny. When a guy's pal is killed, he ought to do something about it."

Coral: "Don't you love me?"

Rip: "That's the tough part of it, but it'll pass. These things do in time. And there's one more thing—I loved him more."

Regardless of these interesting aspects to the story, the reason to watch *Dead Reckoning* is the luminous Lizabeth Scott. While growing up in Scranton, Pennsylvania, the then Emma Matzo had dreams of becoming a great stage actress. She first went to New York and studied at the Alviene School of the Theatre. In 1942 she became Tallulah Bankhead's understudy in the production of Thornton Wilder's *The Skin of Our Teeth* on Broadway. Although a talented young actress by this time, Scott was hired primarily to keep Bankhead in line. "And I think that must have driven her crazy," Scott concluded. The producer's ploy worked—because of the threat of the blonde beauty eclipsing her in the lead, Bankhead never missed a performance. However, Lizabeth did get her chance to shine when the play traveled to Boston. Also at that time, the production changed her name to "Elizabeth." But she went even further and dropped the E. "I decided I needed to make the name more of an attention-grabber," Scott said.

Now a working actress, Scott modeled to make ends meet; one job involved standing before the lens of respected photographer Louise Dahl-Wolfe for *Harper's Bazaar*. Hollywood agent Charles Feldman saw a series of Lizabeth's dramatic photos and took her on as a client. He landed

Lizabeth Scott proves she is indeed a star in *Dead Reckoning.* (GKB Collection)

her a screen test at Warner Bros., but Jack Warner was convinced she would be nothing more than a supporting actress. However, producer Hal Wallis also saw the test and disagreed with Warner; his instinct deemed Scott as star material. This was only one of many disagreements with the studio head, so Wallis left Warner Bros. in 1944 to start his own production company at Paramount. One of his first orders of business was to sign Lizabeth Scott to a contract.

You Came Along (1945) was Scott's first picture for Paramount and with it began the comparisons to Lauren Bacall—their shoulder-length blonde hair, aloof but alluring ways, and signature smoky voices. Both had been models who had started their acting careers on the stage. The studio's publicity department leaned into it and even called Lizabeth "The Threat" to "The Look" of Bacall. Those comparisons would only grow when the newcomer entered the dark world of film noir in 1946 as drifter Toni Marachek in *The Strange Love of Martha Ivers*. It was a small part and she had to share the screen with Barbara Stanwyck, Van Heflin, and Kirk Douglas (in his film debut), but eyes were drawn to Scott. The actress realized, "I fell in love with the lens ... and the lens fell in love with me."

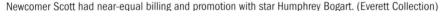

Newcomer Scott had near-equal billing and promotion with star Humphrey Bogart. (Everett Collection)

Whenever Wallis didn't have a part for Scott, he would loan her to other studios to keep her working. Her next picture did more than just bring in a salary—it would be an opportunity to star opposite Humphrey Bogart. *Dead Reckoning* was also her first time in a lead as a femme fatale. While director John Cromwell was less than enthusiastic about hiring the starlet, Columbia was thrilled. The studio rewarded the twenty-five year old with billing and promotion that was just about equal to Bogart's; they are both featured on the movie's posters and advertising. Columbia also provided Lizabeth with star treatment by putting her in the hands of their renowned head of costume design, Jean Louis.

Scott had worked with the great Edith Head during production of *The Strange Love of Martha Ivers*, but Jean Louis was a legitimate designer of haute couture. He brought his vast experience in fashion to the screen and was already famous for Rita Hayworth's costumes in *Gilda*. He'd soon be celebrated for dressing 1950s stars such as Kim Novak, Doris Day, and Marilyn Monroe.

There is something sensual about Jean's designs, a quality that works incredibly well in film noir. Around the time of *Dead Reckoning*, he had returned from a month-long trip to his native Paris, "the first Hollywood stylist to make such a trip, it is said, since

Jean Louis discusses the designs of *Dead Reckoning*'s wardrobe with Scott. (Everett Collection)

before the war," said one syndicated columnist. The design of Scott's costumes came from a mix of high fashion along with references to other films noir. Lizabeth recalled how much work, for the designer and star, went into those costumes: "When I think of all those fittings that I used to have ... you'd fit all these gowns, these suits, these dresses—it would take hours. There would have to be a lot of changes made. Then you'd have to go there the next day. And the next night. And the next night. By the time you got home for dinner, you were truly exhausted. I daresay we worked very hard."

The hard work paid off; Scott's opening gown seduced audiences into theater seats. The plunging black gown became the signature of *Dead Reckoning*, seen in just about every photo and poster promoting the film. However, the director takes his time unveiling the gown. To Lizabeth's credit, Coral Chandler may be the only femme fatale who is introduced with her voice alone. Hero Rip Murdock discovers her at the Sanctuary Club, "Cinderella with a husky voice" ordering a gin fizz at the bar. The camera becomes Bogart's eyes, studying Scott from her peep-toe pumps and shapely calves up to her blonde hair pinned off her face in loose waves. The gown is still not seen in its entirety because a fur coat drapes her shoulders until the couple is seated at a table. But then the coat comes off as she struts around the dance floor singing "Either It's Love or It Isn't."

The timeless design of the gown takes inspiration from the past while looking toward the future. The black halter features a deep neckline, in both front and back, and then skims her figure as it falls to the floor. The dress is daring, almost a throwback to the 1930s and the pre-Code style of Kay Francis. In the more austere 1940s it was news. Columnist Erskine Johnson described the costume from the set in July 1946: "Lizabeth Scott wears a backless and almost frontless evening gown for a scene in *Dead Reckoning*. Designer Jean Louis describes it as his 1948 'umbilicular model.'"

An ongoing challenge for costume designers is predicting fashion, so Louis was declaring this design to be something new. Scott's gown was paired with floating sleeves that left her shoulders bare. In some promotional pictures, she wears full-length gloves so it's possible there was a last-minute decision to uncover her hands. In any case this additional coverage likely helped overcome objections from the Production Code Administration on the gown's otherwise risqué design.

Scott's second gown in *Dead Reckoning* is another showstopper. At one point she answers the door in a smooth, creamy long-sleeved gown with another neckline that

Scott seems like a warrior in this creamy long-sleeved gown accented with a long tassel at its waist. (Everett Collection)

plunges nearly to her waist. The dress has beautiful drape—a blouson top and column skirt snug around the hips. The long dolman sleeves have details that look like sparkling bracelets stacked along the forearms. Additional detail around her waist looks like a coordinating belt that has a dramatic long tassel attached. It's the gown of a goddess, but a goddess who's also a warrior. In that respect, Jean Louis seems to be reaching back to 1940 and Adrian's gown for Katharine Hepburn in *The Philadelphia Story* as inspiration.

Coral is a duplicitous woman who uses clothes to adapt her character and get what she wants. Sometimes she appears as the seductive siren, slinking around in evening gowns. At other times she affects innocence, feigning the qualities of a friend, a girlfriend, or even a potential wife. As she and Murdock get closer, she chooses a pale green skirt suit paired with blouse and snood in a matching fabric. It was one of Scott's costumes highlighted in the press: "Smooth as pale mint ice cream is this tailored suit with its handstitched buttons worn by Lizabeth Scott.... Her French crepe blouse with its print of green, white, and black, complements the suit of soft green, which is a perfect foil for Miss Scott's ash blonde hair. The outfit was created by Columbia's chief stylist, Jean Louis, who is famous for the straight up and down suit skirts he designs to give added height and slimness to the feminine form."

Some of the slimming effect was achieved

Coral attempts to appear more innocent in a pale green skirt suit paired with a blouse and snood in a matching fabric. (Both photos, Everett Collection)

Above: The beret is a popular accessory in film noir, worn by actresses from Lauren Bacall in *To Have and Have Not* to Peggy Cummins in *Gun Crazy* (1950). Below and opposite: The authentic style of Bogart continues in *Dead Reckoning*. (Photos this page, Everett Collection; opposite page, GKB Collection)

by the jacket alone—single-breasted with five fabric-covered buttons that allowed just the bow of the blouse to peek through at the top. Welt pockets also kept the jacket lean and the lines of the ensemble clean.

Another of her more innocent outfits is a short-sleeved striped dress with a bit of peek-a-boo in the bodice. Its design is similar to two costumes from other films noir. The silhouette is like Claire Trevor's opening white dress in *Murder, My Sweet*, but the design also seems to reference Scott's own striped sun suit in *The Strange Love of Martha Ivers*. Coral wears more innocent-looking costumes—the dress and suit—in scenes in which she and Rip are falling for one another.

Scott's last costume of the movie is another suit, but it's broken into two outfits for the final scenes. When Murdock and Coral plan their assault on mobster Martinelli at his club, the audience first sees her in a black mock-neck blouse with long dolman sleeves tucked into a belted striped pencil skirt. She accessorizes the ensemble with a black beret and peep-toe pumps. As she gets ready to go, Coral slips on a slim striped jacket that matches the skirt with four fabric-covered buttons that start at the waist and fasten almost all the way up to the neckline. Especially with the beret, the look is similar to Bacall's iconic suits in both *To Have and Have Not* and *The Big Sleep*.

Bogart had his own recognizable looks in those two movies, which helped him to remain popular with audiences during the post-war years. By this point in the 1940s, he had transcended whatever part he was playing with an authenticity that included his style. Whether the character was Sam Spade, Philip Marlowe, or Rip Murdock, audiences were watching Humphrey Bogart, a view reinforced by the fact that the suits he wore in his pictures were his own. His style had evolved slightly—moving from the striped suits of his earlier pictures like *The Maltese Falcon*, for example, to the dark solid suit, likely navy, that he wears throughout *Dead Reckoning*. The ventless jacket is single-breasted with a two-button closure. The welt pockets keep the lines of the jacket clean, and it's accessorized with a simple white linen pocket square. His trousers were finished with cuffs and paired with a brown leather belt. Bogart reportedly wore suits from Caraceni—Italian tailors who worked with stylish Hollywood stars like Gary Cooper and Tyrone Power. Caraceni suits were known for stronger shoulders, narrow waists, and soft construction. All these design ideas worked well with Bogart's lean frame, perfectly combining toughness with sophistication.

Not everyone, however, was enamored with Bogart's look in *Dead Reckoning*. Hedda Hopper visited the set and then complained in her column: "Humphrey Bogart's clothes in *Dead Reckoning* looked so bad the studio sent for his tailor. Said the director, 'That suit's terrible.' Replied the tailor, 'It's because of your bad lights.' Chimed in Bogey, 'I always look this way.'" A look at

Scott looks pretty in a dress design that seems inspired by the striped sun suit she wore in *The Strange Love of Martha Ivers* and Claire Trevor's white stunner in *Murder, My Sweet*. (Everett Collection)

the film seems to show that all the concerns were addressed. Bogart's suit is fit to perfection.

Dead Reckoning often is accused of being derivative, but it has a lot to offer through its style. Lizabeth Scott's costumes, couture creations from Jean Louis, helped establish the actress' style in film noir. The comparison with Lauren Bacall in the press would often prove unfavorable, but Scott had her own distinct presence on-screen. Her sensual and risqué gowns in *Dead Reckoning* are styled just for her. Her dramatic black halter dress is famous in fashion despite *Dead Reckoning*'s status as a lesser-known noir. The design would have a significant impact on style of the 1970s and 1980s, seen in the work of legends like Halston and Calvin Klein.

Even with all this glamour, Scott remained unconvinced of her own beauty. "I would always say, Lizabeth, you're interesting. But you're not pretty," she once confessed. Considering she's celebrated as a stunning actress of film noir, modern audiences would respectfully disagree.

Coral's con is slowly revealed—her character changes dramatically from the beginning of the film noir to the end. (Top photo, GKB Collection; bottom photo, Everett Collection)

Audrey Totter shows off the elegance of Irene in *Lady in the Lake*. (Everett Collection)

Lady in the Lake

Premiere: January 23, 1947
Director: Robert Montgomery
Costume designer: Irene
Studio: MGM

In 1947 even film noir was a way to say "Happy Holidays." The fact that those season's greetings came from MGM—a studio best known for wholesome family fare like the Andy Hardy series—speaks volumes about the popularity of murder mysteries in the mid-1940s. Based on a book by Raymond Chandler, the screen version of *Lady in the Lake* shifts the setting from summertime to Christmas. The holidays become more than just a backdrop to the story. The opening credits appear on greeting cards accompanied by a medley of Christmas musical selections, from "Jingle Bells" to "God Rest Ye Merry, Gentlemen." The audience is reminded that this is noir only when a gun appears underneath the cards—a gun that might be responsible for a murder. Or two. Or three.

Robert Montgomery directs and also stars as private eye Phillip Marlowe (the spelling of the detective's first name slightly different from the novel). The film is best known for its groundbreaking camera work: It was shot entirely from Marlowe's point of view. As a result, the camera often fixes on actress Audrey Totter as she plays pulp magazine editor Adrienne Fromsett wearing chic costumes by Irene.

Montgomery not only stepped into the shoes of the famous detective, but also took chances as the film's director, an opportunity he had fought for at MGM for several years. "I had a little trouble making this picture," he said at the time. "That is, if you can call eight years of arguing trouble. Nobody seems to want an actor to become a director."

Montgomery was more than an actor; he was one of the studio's biggest stars. He had signed his first contract with Metro in 1929 and was soon paired with its most popular actresses. In 1930 alone he appeared opposite Greta Garbo in *Inspiration*, Norma Shearer in *The Divorcee*,

After a decade of acting in sophisticated comedies, Robert Montgomery proved he could be tough too. (Everett Collection)

and Joan Crawford in *Our Blushing Brides*. MGM leading man Clark Gable may be better known today, but Montgomery was equally in demand during the Art Deco era.

All the sophisticated comedies he made through the Golden Age make it easy to think he completely miscast himself as a tough guy in *Lady in the Lake*. Montgomery, however, was as tough as they come—both mentally and physically. He served as four-time president of the Screen Actors Guild from 1935 to 1938 and from 1946 to 1947, which were challenging times in Hollywood. During his first term, he hired detectives to investigate and help indict organized crime in the industry's labor unions. When World War II erupted and before America was even involved, Montgomery traveled to Europe and volunteered to drive ambulances for the American Field Service. There he helped evacuate wounded soldiers from Paris when it fell to Germany. Once America entered the war, he enlisted in the Navy. Montgomery was involved in action in both the Atlantic and Pacific, including commanding a destroyer during the Normandy invasion. He also commanded PT boats, which gave him the perfect experience for the first film he completed upon his return to Hollywood, John Ford's *They Were Expendable* (1945).

Montgomery had longed for more serious roles as an actor, which made *They Were Expendable* just the film he needed. "The directors shoved a cocktail shaker in my hands and kept me shaking it for years," he said of his work in the 1930s. He had asked MGM head Mayer multiple times for the chance to direct but wasn't taken seriously. Montgomery's lucky break was a literal one—Ford broke his leg with two weeks left in the production, and the studio needed to know whether they should wait for the director to mend or get someone else to finish the film. Without hesitation, Ford said, "Let Montgomery do it." Not only did the former destroyer skipper show himself to be a strong lead in a serious picture, he also finally got the opportunity to helm one himself.

Only a year or so later, Montgomery would be directing again for *Lady in the Lake*. As a director, he made an ambitious choice. Chandler's books tell each story from Marlowe's perspective, so Robert was determined to position the motion picture the same way. With cinematographer Paul Vogel's guidance, the camera became the eyes of the detective as he discovers clues in a suspect's house, climbs out of an automobile accident, receives a beating from a cop, and stares at a shapely blonde secretary (Lila Leeds).

Lady in the Lake became the first use of "subjective camera" throughout an entire film and, not surprisingly, Montgomery and Vogel faced technical challenges. Cameras were large and cumbersome in the 1940s, so having the camera move as a human would be an achievement. "A special, Martian-looking, battery-driven camera had to be built," reported *Los Angeles Times* columnist Jack Sher. Many know the technique from the film noir *Dark Passage* (1947) that came out nine months later, but the technique was used for only part of that picture. Some, like film critic Edwin Schallert, called *Lady in the Lake* "very ingenious" after its premiere, although opinions have grown

Audrey wears Adrienne's Christmas party dress as Montgomery trains his subjective camera on her. (Everett Collection)

more critical over the years.

Montgomery had an entirely new take on Raymond Chandler, whose work shaped some of the best film noir of the 1940s. Although he wrote screenplays—adapting James M. Cain's *Double Indemnity* and crafting an original script for *The Blue Dahlia*—Chandler is revered for his novels, particularly those that follow the adventures of private eye Philip Marlowe. His final book of the '40s, *The Lady in the Lake* in 1943, was adapted for the screen by Steve Fisher, a writer with his own noir pedigree. Fisher had been responsible for the novel *Hot Spot*, which had become *I Wake Up Screaming*, as well as scripts for *Johnny Angel* (1945) and *Dead Reckoning*. Like Chandler and Dashiell Hammett, Fisher got his start writing for pulp magazines. He used that experience to expand the character of Adrienne Fromsett in *Lady in the Lake*, promoting her from a mere assistant at a perfumery in the book to an executive at Kingsby Publications in the movie. Adrienne is a very modern woman, so much so that it's easy to forget 1946 was a time many women were leaving the war workforce and making the transition back to life as home-makers. Audrey Totter makes a perfect Adrienne, the strong, sexy editor who first meets Marlowe as one of her potential authors.

The only time the audience sees Marlowe is in mirrors. This black eye is part of the price he pays while working for Adrienne. (Everett Collection)

The talented Totter was vastly different from the femmes fatales she played in film noir. (Everett Collection)

Totter started her time at MGM in early 1944, but the parts she got were either uncredited or uninspired. Then came the film noir *The Postman Always Rings Twice*, where she stole scenes as Madge, the seductress with a hot seat in a stalled car. She caught John Garfield's eye and, as Eddie Muller writes in *Dark City Dames*, "in under a minute Audrey had audiences forgetting about leading lady Lana Turner." The press said Totter had "the physical wham of a Turner" and also called her "an exceptionally talented actress."

Audrey Totter would make her mark in 1940s noir, with strong performances in *The Unsuspected* and *High Wall* (both 1947) and then in *The Set-Up* and *Tension* (both 1949). Audrey became known for playing sexy, intelligent women with motives that kept audiences guessing—like the complex character of Adrienne in *Lady in the Lake*. Marlowe wonders throughout the film whether she's good or bad.

Postman's director Tay Garnett may have gotten Totter noticed, but it was Montgomery who finally turned her into a star. She had one hell of an opportunity to shine in *Lady in the Lake*. Because the camera was positioned from Marlowe's perspective, Adrienne became a major focus of the film. That much screen time might sound like the opportunity of a lifetime for an actress and it was, but Totter realized the risks involved.

"Just about every actress in town—not just the MGM ones—turned Bob down for the leading lady role," Audrey recalled. "No one wanted to stake her career on so chancy and experimental a project."

At the time, Totter was so new that Montgomery was advised against casting her in such a demanding role. However, she excelled in her screen test. Years of experience in radio with success in everything from soap operas to dramas prepared her for the part in *Lady in the Lake*.

"I already knew how to make love to a microphone," she said, "I just switched to a camera." The approach worked.

"Miss Totter greatly intrigues, reminding at times of Bette Davis and again of Ida Lupino, but being very individual too," wrote Edwin Schallert in the *Los Angeles Times*. Even Hedda Hopper became her cheerleader: "Bob Montgomery handed Metro a star in *Lady in the Lake*. Her name—which I've been screaming for two years—is Audrey Totter."

Because the focus is indeed on Audrey for much of the movie, Montgomery was committed to maximizing her style. Totter recalled: "Bob saw to it that I got grade-A treatment. He told the legendary hair stylist Sydney Guilaroff, 'I want something unusual for Audrey.' And he got it in a succession of pretzel-twist upsweeps that gave my character the proper smart, taut look. The fabulous Irene did the clothes."

Just about the only thing about Adrienne that doesn't keep Marlowe guessing is her style. (Everett Collection)

By 1946, the year that *Lady in the Lake* was in production, Irene Lentz Gibbons had been head of costume design at MGM for four years. Irene, as she was known and credited on all her films, took over the department in 1942 at Louis B. Mayer's request after Adrian retired. The signature style she established as a couturier at her own boutique and later at Bullocks-Wilshire department store continued at Metro. "Her methods of designing are, above all, intelligent," a former Bullocks colleague recalled. Perfectionism was evident in her sharp silhouettes and the sophistication in which she used fabrics and patterns. In contrast to colleagues like Helen Rose, who loved designing for musicals, Irene preferred creating sleek contemporary costumes. She proved herself proficient in the dark world of noir with the trendsetting wardrobe of *The Postman Always Rings Twice*. "Irene-designed clothes are flawless examples of what any well-dressed woman would gladly wear," declared *Chicago Tribune* fashion writer Rea Seeger.

The wardrobe was a dream for Totter. Irene had become renowned for her impeccable tailoring, especially in the skirt suits popular during World War II. In *Lady in the Lake*, Adrienne is a professional woman and her work wardrobe includes two such tailored suits. The suit jackets are constructed without lapels, reflecting the style of men's suits during the war to conserve fabric. The jackets also are designed with nothing superfluous, so details come from a faux lapel in a contrasting color for one and a polka-dot blouse with a matching scarf trailing out of a pocket for the other.

Adrienne's Christmas party dress is similar in its simplicity and structure with strong extended shoulders and accessorized with a smooth metal choker necklace, a pair of matching bangle bracelets, and a lamb fur coat. Her glamorous silk robes—with the same strong shoulders—are more like gowns with their dra-

Glamorous robes help show a softer side of Adrienne as she falls for Phillip Marlowe. (Everett Collection)

matic bell sleeves and beautiful fasteners in front. But their slightly relaxed silhouettes help show a softer side of Adrienne. She lets her hair down only once in the film—while wearing one of these robes. Irene does a superb job of creating a career wardrobe as well as more intimate ensembles that show Adrienne softening once she starts to fall in love with Marlowe.

Like other great Hollywood costume designers, Irene set trends around the world. "Not only does [she] make the clothing worn by the glamorous stars of the screen, but [she] sets the fashion pace for the world of women," Canadian fashion reporter Grace Foley said. MGM was flooded with messages from women wanting to know all the details of costumes from their favorite films. While this had happened in the 1920s and 1930s, those eras featured style that was much more aspirational and often completely unattainable. Largely due to the rationing from the war, 1940s on-screen style was often made more accessible.

"[Irene's] greatest pride of achievement is the thousands of letters from all round the country asking where the dress, suit, or costume in a certain picture can be purchased," Rea Seeger wrote in a *Chicago Tribune* profile of Irene after production had wrapped in 1946. "The influence of

[her] films cannot be underestimated."

While there is no doubting Irene's impact, *Lady in the Lake* premiered at a pivotal moment in fashion history. On February 12, 1947, only eighteen days after the film's release, Christian Dior debuted his New Look in Paris. The Dior haute couture collection was a seismic shift in fashion. It rejected the minimalism and austerity of the war years and embraced an excess of femininity by using more fabric, more frills, more everything. The transition to 1950s style had begun.

The proximity of *Lady in the Lake* to Dior's launch makes this picture all the more important because it represents something of a line of demarcation between the eras. The costumes are a

Adrienne cares for Marlowe after his Christmas Eve car accident. (Everett Collection)

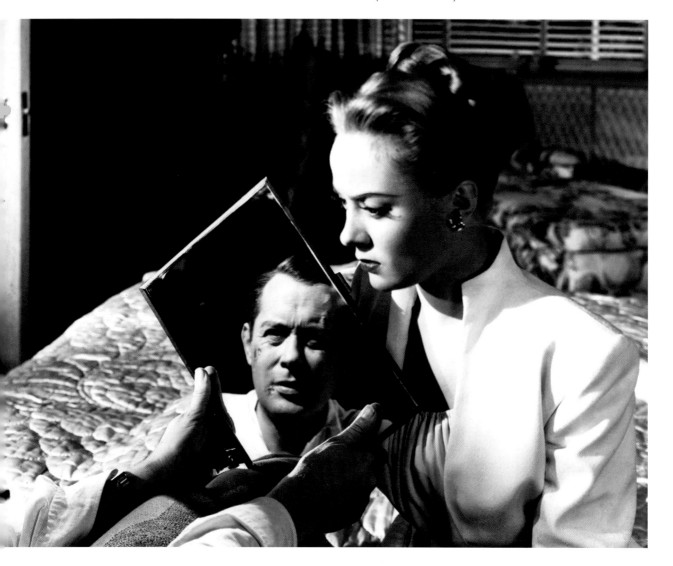

Irene's costumes in *Lady in the Lake* communicate true 1940s style. (Everett Collection)

capsule collection of true 1940s style and the use of subjective camera gives the audience a front-row seat to a fashion show by Irene.

Irene's work was far from out of style, however. That same year, she won the prestigious Neiman Marcus Award and launched her own fashion line, Irene, Inc., while still working at MGM. Her designs might have been perfect for the time, but they were also perfect for all time. The timelessness of her style was proven when costume designer Greg LaVoi dressed Kyra Sedgwick in vintage Irene for the television series *The Closer*. He also briefly resuscitated fashion line Irene, Inc., in 2013 by reproducing original Irene designs in collections that of course included elegant suiting similar to the costumes in *Lady in the Lake*.

Although many don't know this film noir—and some who do criticize it—*Lady in the Lake* deserves to be reconsidered if only for the story of its style.

Jane Greer takes control as femme fatale Kathie Moffat in *Out of the Past*. (Everett Collection)

Out of the Past

Premiere: November 13, 1947
Director: Jacques Tourneur
Costume designer: Edward Stevenson
Studio: RKO

As a film noir, *Out of the Past* paints a world of crime and passion. Robert Mitchum plays Jeff Markham, a private investigator hired to find a gangster's girlfriend after she shoots him and runs off with $40,000. Although a detective is the main character of this film noir, the story is not about solving a crime. Rather it's about Markham's love for a femme fatale—a woman who stays in his soul—and the price he pays for betraying his client to have her. Jane Greer embodies every alluring aspect of Kathie Moffat, playing both a good girl falling in love and a bad girl doing anything to get what she wants. Designer Edward Stevenson is Kathie's co-conspirator, creating costumes that reflect her every mood while leading the audience to completely believe the con.

Jacques Tourneur may not be as well-known a director as contemporaries like John Huston and Billy Wilder, but he had a style all his own. With *Out of the Past*, Jacques Tourneur showed his signature sophisticated artistry in filmmaking. One feature was the mood he was able to create with lighting. In the early 1940s he worked with producer Val Lewton directing a series of low-budget horror films that included *Cat People* (1942) and *I Walked with a Zombie* (1943).

In contrast to Universal's *Dracula* and *Frankenstein*, in which the monsters appeared on-screen, Tourneur used shadows to suggest danger in the darkness and build anxiety in his audiences. His greatest partner was *Cat People*'s cinematographer Nicholas Musuraca, who would collaborate with him again on *Out of the Past*. Musuraca drenches scenes in darkness but also celebrates light enough to make it sparkle. Tourneur's style can be seen, biographer Chris Fujiwara observed, in "the muted gray tone of Musuraca's photography, filled with saturated areas of black and sprinkled with shimmering dots of light reflecting off water and the actors' pupils."

Together, they helped define the look of RKO during the decade as well as the genre of film noir.

Out of the Past begins and ends with scenes flooded with light and the outdoor beauty of Bridgeport, California. But the story quickly becomes sinister, retracing the past from Acapulco to San Francisco as fate closes in, and each revelation along the way takes Markham deeper into the darkness. That blackness had its origin in Daniel Mainwaring's 1946 book *Build My Gallows High*. He had published a series of hard-boiled mysteries in the 1930s under the name Geoffrey Homes, but soon grew tired of simple detective stories. He turned to screenwriting instead and adapted *Gallows*, his final novel, for Tourneur.

Out of the Past is what Fujiwara describes as "a study in power struggles, mistrust, and shifting alliances." No one is who they seem to be and sinister undertones color every conversation. As Markham, Robert Mitchum moves through his mission wearing his familiar trench coat and slouch hat and with a cigarette dangling from his mouth. His performance is understated, a quality Tourneur admired in actors and one he strove to bring out through his films. "Mitchum can be silent and listen to a five-minute speech," the director said. "You'll never lose sight of him and you'll understand that he takes in what is said to him, even if he doesn't do anything." This

A film noir ideal: As detective Jeff Markham, Robert Mitchum is never in a hurry and listens more than he speaks. (Everett Collection)

intensity and calm is central to the character; Jeff is never in a hurry, not even in moments of crisis. It helps the audience believe him to be the "good guy," although they're sometimes uncertain of his intentions.

In contrast, the intentions of Kathie Moffat are always in question. *Out of the Past*'s femme fatale is a complex character. Sometimes Jane Greer gives Kathie the sensuality and spontaneity of a woman falling in love. At other times she's cold, cunning, and ruthless in her need for control. Hers is a layered performance from a young actress who, while relatively new at RKO, had already experienced something of the life of an intrigante.

In 1943 the nineteen year old married singer-actor Rudy Vallee. Decades older than Jane, he saw her as an object of fantasy rather than a wife. Her *Out of the Past* co-star Kirk Douglas recalled, "I loved hearing her stories of her brief marriage to Rudy ... and how he insisted that she wear black panties, black net stockings, and black shoes with heels so high she teetered." Noir expert Eddie Muller learned from Greer that in addition to dressing her in lingerie, "[Vallee] even had her auburn locks dyed jet-black, trying to create a carbon copy of Hedy Lamarr, one of his unconquered fetish figures."

Rudy wasn't the only questionable character who entered Greer's life in 1943. After seeing her photo in *LIFE* magazine, Howard Hughes had also pursued her and signed the starlet to one of his per-

Greer models a costume for *Out of the Past* that was used only in promotion. (Everett Collection)

sonal contracts that same year. However, beyond the acting classes set up for all of Howard's girls, Greer was largely ignored and not cast in any Hollywood productions. She ended up in court to get herself out of both bad relationships.

Greer finally found real work at RKO but at first only in the most minor of roles at the major-minor studio. She seemed stuck in B pictures until the gods sent Joan Harrison to the rescue. Harrison had worked extensively with Alfred Hitchcock, starting in 1933 as his assistant and evolving into a brilliant screenwriter on pictures ranging from *Jamaica Inn* (1939) and *Rebecca* to *Suspicion* and *Saboteur* (1942). She then became a producer—at the time one of only three female producers in Hollywood—with Universal's film noir *Phantom Lady* (1944). *Nocturne*, a 1946 noir, would be Harrison's first production at RKO. Joan almost immediately had her eye on Jane and, thinking it would open up opportunities for the actress, advised that her hair return to its natural auburn. *They Won't Believe Me* and *Out of the Past*, both released in 1947, would be her reward. In the latter she displayed natural chemistry with Robert Mitchum that made it easy to understand Jeff's obsession with Kathie.

Los Angeles Times film critic Edwin Schallert smartly observed, "It took a woman's discerning eye to discover Jane Greer as a real actress in the movies."

That talent would soon be recognized by the studio's new production head. "Jane Greer is

When Kathie meets Jeff Markham her Acapulco wardrobe projects innocence, as with this light-colored dress with a sweetheart neckline. (Greenbriar Collection)

Kathie wears this summery ensemble when she and Jeff kiss for the first time. (Everett Collection)

the new white hope at RKO," declared columnist Sheilah Graham. "Her boss, Dore Schary, predicts big things for her—based on her two latest movie performances." Of course, she would exceed all expectations. *Out of the Past* established her as a leading lady for the next decade.

As Kathie Moffat, Jane built her performance on two important insights from Tourneur. Greer recalled, "Our director, Jacques Tourneur, was French and didn't speak English very well.... 'I'll tell you what I want,' he explained. 'Eem-pass-seve. Do you know what eem-pass-seve means?' I replied, 'Yes, I know what impassive means.'"

This was the origin of the stoicism of her character, even when slapped hard across the face by Whit Sterling (Kirk Douglas). The other part of Tourneur's direction explained both the character and the movie itself: "First half: good girl. Last half: bad girl." As a result, Greer gave the audience two sides of the same woman: one who was in love with Jeff and the other who loved using him—and other men—to get what she wanted. Each side had a distinctly different wardrobe suiting her mood with each man in each location, from Acapulco to San Francisco.

Edward Stevenson, RKO's head costume designer, expertly constructed Kathie's wardrobes. Stevenson had a family connection to Tourneur—he created his first gown in film for the silent *The White Moth* (1924), which was produced and directed by Jacques' father, Maurice. From that point on, the designer built his career both on and off the screen. He worked at MGM, Fox, and Warner Bros.–First National, and then left the studio system in the early 1930s to open his own shop in Hollywood. There he worked as both a costume designer and a fashion designer known for his fresh ideas and solid craftsmanship. In 1935 Stevenson accepted a position at RKO and focused once again on film. Later, he replaced Bernard Newman as head of costume design.

Falling in love, Kathie wears girlish ruffles and hair combed back to reveal Jeff's gift of jade and silver earrings. (Everett Collection)

"Edward Stevenson [believed] that the woman is first," said features writer Mary Hampton, "and the clothes should bend to glorify her." He would show this time and time again, especially for femmes fatales Claire Trevor in *Murder, My Sweet* and Jane Greer in *Out of the Past*.

As Tourneur dictated, the first half of the film focuses on the innocent side of Kathie Moffat, a guarded woman who can't help falling in love. Her Acapulco wardrobe reflects this innocence from the start. "For my first appearance, I walk into the saloon out of the sunlight wearing a big picture hat while soft, romantic music plays," Jane remembered. She wears a white, fitted day dress with shoulder pads giving structure to delicate cap sleeves. The sweetheart neckline is accented on each side with two sparkling pins. Beyond this, she keeps jewelry to a minimum—just a single gold link bracelet with a charm—and initially refuses Jeff's gift of earrings made of jade and pure silver.

The pair next meet at night, but her light summery look is very similar to her first. The differences show in the details—a scoop neckline and a belted peplum that drops into another layer of her skirt. Her accessories include gloves and a single strap satchel with metallic monograms of her initials. While she wears this dress they share their first kiss on the beach, beautifully lit by

Musuraca. "When Jane gets within embracing distance," observed columnist Will Jones, "you can see the moonlight catching moist highlights on her lip, which look smooth and chewy as a Fanny Farmer caramel." Her third look in Mexico is by far the most romantic and intimates that she's fallen in love. "Then she comes along like school is out," Jeff observes as she bounds toward him barefoot on the beach. Ruffles everywhere—starting along the scoop neckline of her bishop-sleeve blouse—emphasize her girlishness. The blouse tucks into a high-waisted skirt with more ruffles down the front and along the hem. For the first time her hair is pulled back off her face, which allows the audience to see she's now wearing the earrings Jeff bought for her the day they met.

Their move to San Francisco leads to a much darker time and a wardrobe to match. At first the two are still in love, although her clothes—a black fur coat with a pencil skirt and heels—suggest a more serious mood. The real transition comes when Jeff's former partner Jack Fisher (Steve Brodie) trails Kathie from the racetrack. She wears a strong monochromatic look—a fitted jacket with princess seams, buttons all the way up the front, and a hood draped behind her. The jacket hits the high hip of a matching pencil skirt.

"Why don't you break his head, Jeff," Kathie suggests coldly, revealing her true nature for the first time. Her round purse holds items besides a powder puff: a record of the

The femme fatale reveals her true nature in a hooded suit.
(Both photos, Everett Collection)

stolen $40,000 in her savings account and a gun. She stands steely-eyed as she shoots Fisher and watches his lifeless body hit the floor.

Upon her return to San Francisco after a visit to Whit, Kathie shows she's as bad as can be. She's now Sterling's surrogate and helps set up Jeff in a frame. As she orchestrates it all, her ensemble is distinctly different from anything she had worn before. One can sense her power and control, wearing a broad-shouldered mink coat over a black velvet gown with thin spaghetti straps and a tiered skirt. Its biggest accessory is a bold round brooch right in the center of the bodice. Delicate drop earrings are shown off by her hair in an ornate updo, a style unlike her earlier long loose romantic waves.

While Whit Sterling's surrogate, Kathie wears a distinctly darker wardrobe. (Both photos, Everett Collection)

Back at Whit's house in Lake Tahoe, Kathie once again dresses for darkness. She starts with a full-length, long-sleeved robe belted at the waist that almost has the feel of a trench coat. In this robe, she sends Joe Stefanos (Paul Valentine) off to kill Jeff, but the hit man is killed instead. For that mistake, she takes a sharp slap across the face from Whit right before he makes a promise to kill her.

"Cheer up, Kathie, you'll get out of it all right," Jeff predicts as he walks out the door. Pragmatic girl that she is, she decided the solution is to kill Whit too and put herself in charge. In her triumph, she then wears her most powerful ensemble yet: a long fitted coat with princess seams and three big buttons that fasten from her bust down to her cinched waist. Her hair is completely covered by a solid snood coordinated with the coat.

"Don't you see, you have only me to make deals with now," she tells Jeff. "Well, build my gallows high, baby," he says before they kiss for the last time.

Out of the Past is a film noir with a love story at its heart, but that heart is black. Kathie Moffat used style to seduce, to conceal, to appease, to dominate—all via costumes designed by Edward Stevenson. Just as the film begins with light and descends into darkness, so does the wardrobe of the femme fatale. Stevenson's work in *Out of the Past* was so popular that it increased promotion of his fashion designs, which included bridal collections sold across the country and modeled by RKO stars like Jane Russell and Jane Greer. After the premiere of *Out of the Past*, the press celebrated his talent: "Stevenson, a young man with a flair for clothes that are young, never forgets his mission: to help educate the public taste; to design clothes that are simple, wearable, and in character; to do his part in the industry's immense program of entertainment; and to do it well."

Kathie's final costume, a dramatic full coat and snood, communicates she's now the one in charge. (Everett Collection)

Arguably the most famous costume from *The Lady from Shanghai*, Rita Hayworth's strapless satin and lace gown was used only in promotion and not seen in the film. (GKB Collection)

The Lady from Shanghai

Premiere: June 9, 1948
Director: Orson Welles
Costume designer: Jean Louis
Studio: Columbia

If there were such a thing as surreal noir, *The Lady from Shanghai* would be it. Orson Welles exerted extensive creative control as the film's writer, director, and producer and gave it his distinct artistic voice. However, much of the production was yet at the mercy of Columbia Pictures and its head, Harry Cohn. Dueling decisions over editing, lighting, and locations still delivered some of what Welles wanted, which he referred to as the "queer" quality of a "bad dream." The characters might be the most unsettling part of the film, beginning with Rita Hayworth as blonde femme fatale Elsa Bannister, a seductress who is about as bad as bad can get.

Orson Welles helped shape film noir through the 1940s. *Citizen Kane* stands as a giant in movie history, including for its impact on noir. This proto-noir possesses an ominous mood, a story told in sophisticated flashback, dramatic cinematography that is often more shadow than light, and characters who fail to find happy endings. Welles followed *Citizen Kane* with *Journey into Fear*, *The Stranger*, and then *The Lady from Shanghai*, which was based on Sherwood King's 1938 novel *If I Die Before I Wake*.

The extensive creative control Columbia granted to Welles didn't prevent Harry Cohn's numerous interventions. One major change came immediately. Orson had conceived of *Shanghai* as a B picture and wanted to cast an unknown French actress, whom he had under personal contract, as the lead. But Cohn envisioned it differently and named Rita Hayworth as the female lead. *The Lady from Shanghai* mushroomed into a major production; after all, Rita wasn't just a star at the studio, she was *the* star.

Rita had been working in Hollywood since the 1930s, but it wasn't until the 1940s that she really made an impact. Along with the rest of the world, Welles had become infatuated with

Hayworth after a glimpse of the now-famous *LIFE* magazine photo of the siren kneeling on satin sheets in a black lace and white silk slip. "I saw that fabulous still in *LIFE* magazine," Orson recalled. "And that's when I decided: When I come back [from shooting *It's All True* in Brazil], that's what I'm going to do!" They had never met but, true to form and confident as ever, Welles started telling people he was going to marry Rita Hayworth.

After much persistence from Welles, Rita consented to marry him in September 1943. But by March 1946—when *The Lady from Shanghai* was in production—Hayworth had officially separated from Welles and moved into a home in the Brentwood section of Los Angeles. Reconciliation interrupted their estrangement, however, when the director again focused his attention solely on the star during filming. Their relationship provides fascinating subtext to the screenplay, which is filled with double meaning. Rita exhibits real emotion on the yacht as Elsa urgently pleads with Michael, played by Welles, "You've just got to stay."

As with many films released during Hollywood's Golden Age, publicity for *The Lady from Shanghai* concentrated on its style; in fact, style stands above all else in this picture, with Jean

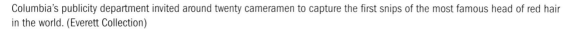

Columbia's publicity department invited around twenty cameramen to capture the first snips of the most famous head of red hair in the world. (Everett Collection)

Louis' costumes—dominated by black and white—calibrated for every location and occasion. Even murder.

Shanghai style begins with Rita's famous head of hair. The news came in shock waves: Not only would her hair be cut, it would be colored as well. Reactions were mixed, with many in Hollywood quick to accuse Welles of ulterior motives; gossip columns had labeled him controlling, and many thought he changed her look simply because he could. But the director had reasons behind the gambit.

"She was going to play a kind of person she'd never been on the screen," Welles explained in conversations with director Peter Bogdanovich. "She couldn't come on as the well-established pinup; she needed a whole new look." The process of achieving that look began, with each stage fed to the

Rita transformed, with her new topaz blonde hair cut into the cinema swirl to play femme fatale Elsa Bannister. (GKB Collection)

media. Artists submitted sketches of possible styles that would fit both the star and her character. Then shades of hair were sampled and scrutinized to find the best for her complexion.

Helen Hunt, the stylist responsible for Rita's auburn tresses, was yanked back from her honeymoon in New York to work on the star when all decisions had been made. Hayworth's hair would be cut into a feathered bob called the "cinema swirl" and her hair color lightened to a bright topaz blonde. Columbia's publicity department worked overtime and invited members of the press, including twenty cameramen, to cover the initial few snips of the most famous head of red hair in the world. Reactions were mixed, although most in Hollywood continued to mourn the loss of Rita's trademark mane. So did some fans across the country, including those from the University of Wisconsin League of Redheads, who wanted her back among them.

Columbia gave its approval, but Harry Cohn remained furious throughout production. "It wasn't just hair, it was a studio asset, a valuable piece of property," said Hayworth biographer Barbara Leaming. When viewing the rushes, Cohn would continue to complain to Rita, "He's ruined you—he cut your hair off!"

Princess Rosaleen—Elsa's deception begins in an innocent white crepe dress scattered with polka dots. (GKB Collection)

Hayworth's hair was but the beginning of the style story of *The Lady from Shanghai*. Rita's entire look was of paramount importance and assigned to the studio's head costume designer, Jean Louis. The couturier had already made history dressing Hayworth, his strapless "Put the Blame on Mame" gown for Hayworth in *Gilda* being among his most lasting achievements. Louis loved working with Rita and gave *The Lady from Shanghai* his entire attention, outfitting the star in glamorous costumes that fit each location of the film noir.

The story begins like a fairy tale in New York City with Welles' character, Michael, meeting Elsa in a horse-drawn carriage in Central Park. Hayworth's first costume is a dress fit for a princess "made of white crepe with scattered black polka dots," wrote Eileen Callahan in the *Daily News*. "The draped bodice has a deep, wide [sweetheart] neckline. The twisted cape sleeves fasten at the back belt [and] are caught in at each side of the neckline." Everything about the scene is romantic as Michael rescues her from harm. He even calls her "Rosaleen, fair Rosaleen ... a gorgeous romantic" name for the innocent image he has of Elsa. Michael then calls her "Princess," even as he starts to learn of her dark past along the Chinese coast: born to White Russian parents in "the second wickedest city in the world," Zhifu, then working her way through even more wickedness in Macau all the way up the coast to Shanghai.

"You need more than luck in Shanghai," she says with a hint of the real woman hidden within. Welles hated the film's opening scenes in the park, telling Bogdanovich, "When I think of it, my flesh crawls. The whole sequence has no flavor." However, that lack of flavor is exactly the point. It lulls the audience into thinking that Elsa is a victim and this is a love story. Instead, one should wonder why she hides a gun in her clutch.

The film then moves onto the yacht of her husband, Arthur Bannister (Everett Sloane). Fittingly named for the mythical enchantress Circe, the boat travels from New York through the Panama Canal to the tropical waters of Acapulco Bay. Elsa's costumes take on a distinctly nautical feel as they get ready to set sail. She meets Michael wearing a white captain's hat, a dark double-breasted blazer with gold buttons over white shorts, and white platform strappy sandals. She wears almost an inverse of this outfit in another scene as she stands at the helm of the *Circe* in a black captain's hat with a black halter bikini and shorts paired with a creamy peacoat. Once they're moored offshore, Elsa gracefully high dives off a Mexican cliff while George Grisby (Glenn Anders), Bannister's law partner, watches through his telescope. His voyeurism continues as she climbs out of the water and suns herself on the rocks in a shiny satin one-piece swimsuit.

The real captain of the ship—once they set sail on *Circe*, Elsa wears a number of ensembles that have a nautical feel. (Everett Collection)

Elsa seduces in every costume, especially in her sun suit and her sculpted swimsuit. (Both photos, Everett Collection)

The black bodice is similar to Rita's famous *Gilda* gown and only significantly differs in a single asymmetrical strap that ties at her shoulder.

Hayworth may be at her most beautiful in the scene in which she's lying on the yacht as night falls, wearing a bandeau bikini top and shorts styled like sailor's pants while smoking a cigarette and singing. Due to Rita's popularity in musicals, Cohn asked to see her sing, at least a little, in *The Lady from Shanghai*. He also demanded more and more close-ups, and Welles worked with cinematographer Rudolph Maté on these requests back on the Columbia sound stages. The edits from locations to studio shots give *Shanghai* that surreal flavor.

Maté had been renowned for lighting that captures what one critic called "the spiritual dimension of facial expression" ever since his work on *The Passion of Joan of Arc* (1928). He knew Rita well, having been behind the camera for her first screen test and then lighting her to perfection in *Gilda*. Together again, he makes her luminous with makeup by Bob Schiffer and hair styled by Hunt.

Once in Acapulco, Rita's wardrobe evolves with the extreme heat of Mexico. On a "picnic"—an arduous journey through the jungle that feels like a scene from Joseph Conrad's *Heart of Darkness*—she wears a cap-sleeved dress over print silk shorts and a bra top. A beige belt with an attached pocket (is her gun inside?) holds the dress open so it acts as a lightweight cover-up. The heat only gets worse when the "sharks"—Bannister, Grisby, and Elsa—start to attack one another. During one of Bannister's drunken jabs, he tells Michael, "You oughta hear the [story] about how Elsa got to be my wife." Making it clear there is something very damaging in her past, she responds, "You want me to tell him what you've got on me, Arthur?"

Elsa plays the victim again in the streets of Acapulco as "Amado Mío," one of the songs from *Gilda*, plays in the night. Once again she dons a dress that inspires romance: a strapless gown made of sheer white marquisette scattered with rhinestones and a matching capelet with a small Peter Pan collar. Louis cleverly constructs the dress for movement; the fabric floats as Elsa runs down the street.

In San Francisco the surrealism hits its peak, and Elsa reveals her true character. Locations range from the Steinhart Aquarium to the Mandarin Theatre in Chinatown to the Crazy House at an abandoned amusement park. From this point on, her costumes are very different from the ones that seduced Michael. Much of the romance reflected in the earlier styles is replaced with power—Elsa's power over men in pursuit of money. She wears the perfect costume for a villainess: a black crepe gown with short sleeves floating off strong shoulders and a molded bodice that drops into a pleated skirt embroidered with gold beads. The audience sees the shift in her character in this dress when she comes upon Sidney Broome (Ted de Corsia), Bannister's private detective, after he's been shot.

Jean Louis fits Rita in a romantic white marquisette gown sprinkled with rhinestones. (Everett Collection)

213

Her complete calm as he lies dying is chilling.

In an interview with John Kobal, Jean Louis commented on designing for Hayworth: "With Rita you always had to design to show off her body—not her legs, but her body; I mean, you couldn't put her in a business suit. Not because the studio would have objected, but because that was her personality. Rita Hayworth was known for that, for being a beautiful woman, and people didn't want to see Rita Hayworth in a suit."

But the costume designer did just that multiple times in *The Lady from Shanghai*. In fact, suits are used in key moments, including the final scenes. Elsa first wears a fitted gray skirt suit to trial when she is subpoenaed and called to the stand. It's accessorized with a brooch, elaborate veiled hat, and white ermine wrap. Her suit, minus those embellishments, likely inspired the same-color suits in Alfred Hitchcock's *The Man Who Knew Too Much* and *Vertigo*.

When Michael escapes from the courthouse, Elsa, wearing a mink coat over a black wool suit with satin trim, chases him to Chinatown and into the opera house. In this suit, gun in hand, she hisses her confession to Michael and tries to slither away af-

The look of a killer: a black crepe gown with a molded bodice that drops into a pleated skirt embroidered with gold beads. (Both photos, Everett Collection)

ter the film's climactic shootout in the amusement park's Hall of Mirrors.

Hayworth wanted the opportunity to prove she could be more than just a love goddess in film; Orson Welles granted her wish with *The Lady from Shanghai*, changing her image in both the character she played and her on-screen appearance. Although Elsa is described as a redhead in the book, Welles wanted the audience to expect something different from Rita in this film. Different is what they got—that champagne blonde hair was the only thing about the character that was light; any sweetness was a smoke screen for a cunning killer. Among femmes fatales, Elsa may be the worst; she's effective because she maintains an aura of innocence. Jean Louis' costumes enhance the illusion and help Elsa accomplish her act. It's a wardrobe dominated by black and white, but the movie is all about illusion and shades of gray.

As the film was shot during 1946 and 1947, the costumes still reflected much of the style of the war years, especially with the strong shoulder lines and skirt suits. Both Hayworth's hair and costumes were covered extensively in the press and used to promote the film, including a now famous strapless black lace and satin gown that appeared only in advertising.

There are layers of meaning in this surreal film noir—including the end of the marriage of Orson and Rita—and so much of the story is told with style.

Elsa wears skirt suits at the film noir's finish—a gray suit to defend Michael in court and a black suit to kill him. (Everett Collection)

Marilyn Monroe made a breakthrough playing intrigante Angela Phinlay in *The Asphalt Jungle* (Getty Collection)

The Asphalt Jungle

Premiere: June 8, 1950
Director: John Huston
Costume designer: Helen Rose
Studio: MGM

Filmed in fall 1949, John Huston's *The Asphalt Jungle* marked a turning point for film noir. Critics celebrated its authenticity and proclaimed it darker than anything seen before in the decade. The movie almost feels like a documentary in its realism, and it defied the Production Code's command to not show how to commit a crime. The central story: steal a half-million dollars' worth of jewelry. And the audience saw how to do it, from the inception of the idea to the hiring of a team to the robbery itself to the consequences and aftermath. Huston depicted this timeline so effectively that he made the heist a new form of film noir, one that would influence movies like *Rififi* (1955), *Ocean's 11* (1960), and *Reservoir Dogs* (1992).

The Asphalt Jungle was based on a novel by W. R. Burnett, who had written some of the best gangster novels and scripts including *Little Caesar* (1930), *Scarface*, *High Sierra*, and *This Gun for Hire*. Huston and Ben Maddow adapted the story, and the script and direction of *The Asphalt Jungle* resisted any sensationalism. The minimalist approach made the audience believe. These men are not cartoon gangsters. They seem like professionals doing their jobs, just trying to make a living. "*The Asphalt Jungle* offered an underworld of struggling laborers, alienated loners, even honorable family men," said Eddie Muller. Huston viewed the criminals in this way, and his own words are articulated by the character of Alonzo Emmerich as played by Louis Calhern: "Crime is only a left-handed form of human endeavor."

These men are tough, but show vulnerability through their affection for family and friends. The women are tough, too, although the leading ladies have very different motivations. Sweet chorus girl Doll Conovan (Jean Hagen) is completely dedicated to Dix Handley (Sterling Hayden), the caper's gunman. Doll does everything for love. The other woman in *The Asphalt*

Monroe exudes many emotions as voluptuary Angela. (GKB Collection)

Jungle, Emmerich's young mistress Angela Phinlay, is played by an actress who would transform the 1950s and fashion forever—Marilyn Monroe. Angela acts entirely in her own interests. The novel describes Angela as a "mercenary trollop." As Angela, Monroe exudes many emotions in her two scenes on-screen, especially her final interaction with the police.

"In two and a half minutes and after only two takes," said Monroe biographer Donald Spoto, "Marilyn created Angela not as a cartoon-like simpleton but a voluptuary torn between fear, childlike loyalty, brassy self-interest, and weary self-loathing." MGM head costume designer Helen Rose helped Marilyn make the most of those brief moments in the movie and established a style for Monroe that would also characterize her offscreen.

Marilyn had starred in the minor Columbia picture *Ladies of the Chorus* (1948) and appeared in a walk-on role in the Marx Brothers' *Love Happy* (1949) for United Artists. But *The Asphalt Jungle* was considered her big break. Before playing Angela, "Marilyn Monroe was just another blonde trying to crash Hollywood," reporter Lydia Lane said in 1952. "After that picture she was a star."

The opportunity presented itself thanks to the devotion of her agent and lover Johnny Hyde, who used his connections at MGM to land Marilyn an audition with Huston even though her face didn't resemble the character Burnett had drawn in his novel—a girl with red hair and yellowish-brown eyes. However, Monroe did possess other attributes that were right on the money. Angela was "slenderly but voluptuously made; and there was something about her walk—something lazy, careless and insolently assured—that was impossible to ignore."

Monroe lay on the floor to read her scene for the director, but did such a terrible job she begged for another chance. Unfortunately, the second attempt failed to improve upon the first, although the courage behind her ask impressed the director. After years of not succeeding in Hollywood, her ambition was now tinged with desperation. Her set of struggles and experience gave her a genuine understanding of Angela, whose wantonness helps her get what she desires. Marilyn's famous figure also helped her get what she wanted. As Huston watched her walk from MGM's Thalberg building, he reportedly said, "Look at the ass on that little girl."

Despite two poor auditions, director John Huston saw Marilyn's potential and launched her career. (Both photos, GKB Collection)

All of this made her "Angela to a T."

As with *The Maltese Falcon*, Huston took all his direction from the novel and lifted much of the dialogue for the script from its pages. However, the wardrobe for Angela was another matter and relied on the vision of MGM costume designer Helen Rose. Although she gained renown for designing glamorous gowns, particularly confections made of chiffon, she understood the world of noir better than most. Rose lived an exciting life from an early age. She had already been designing clothes when she leveraged her good grades in grammar school to attend the Chicago Academy of Fine Arts. This was the era of Prohibition and with so many clubs in the city, the school was often scouted for talent. Helen's unique sketches earned her employment designing for exotic burlesque shows. She created sexy and often skimpy costumes for the showgirls, learning the value of a strategically placed bugle bead. Perhaps most intriguing, 1920s Chicago meant these clubs were run by Al Capone. Little did these club managers know that their designer was only sixteen years old.

In 1929, after years of working in mob-run Chicago, Rose moved to Los Angeles. Life

Helen Rose started her career designing costumes for showgirls in 1920s Chicago. (Everett Collection)

was sunny at first, but her success led her to experience the dark side of the studio system. Her early days included designing for Fanchon and Marco, producers of national live stage shows that played in theaters before movie screenings. These shows became important testing grounds for talent like Judy Garland and Doris Day, who would go on to become big stars. Working with Fanchon and Marco gave Helen the platform to get noticed. Executives at 20th Century Fox were among her admirers, and they hired her—then fired her—then hired her again as a costume designer. The instability and volatility of Hollywood made her never want to work in the industry again, but Louis B. Mayer soon made Rose an

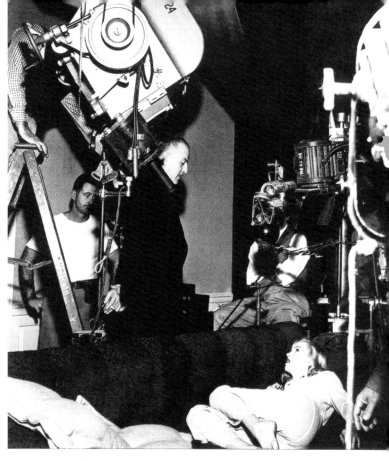

offer she couldn't refuse. In 1943 he hired her as one of MGM's costume designers. However, he did it without consulting the studio's head designer Irene, which set Helen up to suffer severe internal studio politics. After six years it was Irene's turn to be fired, and Rose became the head of costume design.

MGM had always been known for glamour, and Helen easily achieved Mayer's one standing order to "just make them look beautiful." She worked well with stars, and many of the biggest were also personal friends. Helen considered Lana Turner, Elizabeth Taylor, and Grace Kelly to be like sisters.

Every so often, however, a production like *The Postman Always Rings Twice* ran contrary to the studio's standard style voice. And every so often an actress would bring additional challenges. Both would be true with *The Asphalt Jungle* and Marilyn Monroe. Later Monroe films such as *Gentlemen Prefer Blondes* (1953) and *The Seven Year Itch* (1955) have made such an impact on fashion that it's hard to remember a time when she wasn't an icon. It's also hard to remember that style didn't come naturally to her. As Rose recalled: "Marilyn Monroe was a very kind, gentle girl, but she was—figure-wise—no designer's dream, nor was she a 'fashion plate.' Somehow she always looked like she had come in from a windstorm or as Ann Straus, who handled fash-

Rose designed a flirty but simple striped top and matching pants to highlight Angela's femininity and youth. (Both photos, GKB Collection)

221

This publicity photo of the black dress shows how well its less-structured design works for Monroe. (GKB Collection)

ion publicity, would say, 'Like an unmade bed.'"

Johnny Hyde was aware of this and asked Helen to dress Marilyn with class, an unnecessary request for anyone who knew the costume designer. In addition, MGM already had a history of stunning blonde stars going back to Marilyn's idol Jean Harlow; Marilyn was now being compared with Harlow's successor Lana Turner. The similarity was encouraged by the studio, which had Monroe's hair styled like Lana's for *The Asphalt Jungle*.

The up-and-coming actress wasn't pleased. "I don't like it a bit when they say I resemble Lana Turner," she said after the movie's premiere. "I think I have looks and personality of my own." No one would agree more than her costume designer. Perhaps due to Marilyn's experience modeling swimsuits, Rose saw a resemblance between Monroe and Chicago showgirls who were more comfortable wearing less. Rose even tried putting Monroe in one of Turner's cocktail suits because they shared the same measurements at the time, but thought she "only looked untidy and cheap."

Helen knew she had to do something different for the starlet. She maintained that Monroe "looked much better in a skimpy towel than in expensive, high fashion clothes." One of the costumes in *The Asphalt Jungle* seems inspired by this notion. Her black off-the-shoulder dress was designed in such a way that it seemed both formal and casual, almost as if Marilyn was rolling out of bed. Monroe was photographed in the dress in numerous poses for MGM's publicity, many capturing the feeling of the actress undressing with the garment slipping down her shoulders. Rose smartly accentuated Marilyn's 37-24-36 figure in the design—ruching around her bust, cinching her small waist, and hugging her hips and derriere with a slight gathering of fabric in the back. The longer length and asymmetrical hemline, higher in the front than in the back, spoke to style that was then moving into the 1950s. Rose finished the costume with key pieces of jewelry—a choker necklace and bracelet designed by Joseff of Hollywood—that represented expensive gifts for Angela from Emmerich.

Equally enticing is the ensemble Marilyn wears in her first scene. After the movie's premiere, the media was abuzz about her breathtaking appearance. Angela's introduction in the book doesn't suggest a particular costume nor how seductive the moment could be, but John Huston recognized the power of Marilyn Monroe. Beautifully lit by Harold Rosson, who had been married to Jean Harlow, Marilyn slowly opens her eyes as she awakens under the gaze of her lover. There's nothing revealing about her outfit, yet Monroe's sultry look makes the audience understand at once why Emmerich has sacrificed so much for this girl.

Rose designed a flirty but simple striped top and matching pants that work to emphasize the character's youth. Diagonal stripes flatter and highlight her femininity. Her jewelry is limited to a diamond brooch pinned near the shawl collar, another expensive gift from Emmerich. As Angela breaks his kiss to pad off to bed barefoot, locking the door behind her, he turns one of her bejeweled mules around in his hands. He contemplates everything he has done to keep her, which in the novel included "money by the handfuls," a car, a mink coat, and that jewelry—gifts that cost more than $100,000 and drove him to a crime that ended in catastrophe.

Helen Rose's off-the-shoulder dress in *The Asphalt Jungle* was a template for early Marilyn Monroe style, including this design from Oleg Cassini for the premiere of *Monkey Business* (1952). (Everett Collection)

223

Above and opposite: The design of Monroe's legendary pink dress in the color noir *Niagara* (1953) takes some inspiration from her costume in *The Asphalt Jungle*. (Above photo, Everett Collection; opposite photo, GKB Collection)

The Asphalt Jungle is admired for the authenticity of its stars' performances, and Marilyn deserves special attention for hers. With only two scenes, the actress made this film noir her breakthrough under the skilled guidance of John Huston. Beyond her acting skills, which are far too often underappreciated, she stood out with her style. She had, according to reporter Harold Hefferman writing in *The Pittsburgh Press*, a "sensuous brand of blonde appeal and a provocative figure that is dressed—or undressed—to the hilt in this movie."

Marilyn Monroe may be best known for her partnership with costume designer Travilla at 20th Century Fox, but Helen Rose proved an early contributor to her legendary look. Her off-the-shoulder dress in *The Asphalt Jungle* became a favorite silhouette of the actress offscreen. In fact, fashion designer Ceil Chapman would recreate the design again and again for the star, including a version in white for her famous *LIFE* magazine cover in April 1952. Hollywood, always hungry for a new star, found it in Marilyn. Her success in *The Asphalt Jungle* would lead to *Don't Bother to Knock* (1952) followed by *Niagara*—three films noir that put her on the path to becoming an icon.

225

C.B.DeMILLE

Gloria Swanson is ready for her close-up as the tragic Norma Desmond in *Sunset Boulevard*. (Everett Collection)

Sunset Boulevard

Premiere: August 10, 1950
Director: Billy Wilder
Costume designer: Edith Head
Studio: Paramount

Few films capture the feel of Hollywood better than director Billy Wilder's noir *Sunset Boulevard*. While much of the movie seems almost dreamlike—starting with voiceover narration courtesy of a character already dead—in many ways it couldn't be more true to life. Wilder wove fact with fiction at every turn of the production—from its classic Los Angeles locations to the actors to its story of a fallen star. Even its costume design with its deep history between Edith Head and star Gloria Swanson adds to the surrealism. Costumes, always important in a film, prove vital in *Sunset Boulevard*. With Head's help, Swanson transforms herself into Norma Desmond.

The realism in *Sunset Boulevard* began with Wilder's search for the right actress to play Desmond. He approached Mae West, Mary Pickford, and Pola Negri, but each expressed concern that her life had come too close to that of Desmond—a former and now faded great star. In contrast, Swanson did not resemble the character. She had developed into an energetic and savvy businesswoman who was always working. Through her success in acting, she became a producer and one of the first women to finance her own productions. And through her success as a producer, she evolved into an entrepreneur, most notably designing fashions and running an apparel company in New York.

Sunset Boulevard seems all the more real because of how much Swanson's life intersects with characters in the film. Even minor characters are familiar faces—fellow silent-screen stars Buster Keaton, H.B. Warner, and Anna Q. Nilsson make a group appearance at Norma's card game. Actress-turned-gossip columnist Hedda Hopper also makes a cameo at the end of the movie. Two of Swanson's co-stars have the deepest connection to her—Erich von Stroheim and Cecil B.

DeMille. Stroheim plays Max Von Mayerling, Norma's butler who also had been her husband and movie director. Max is described in the film as one of the great directors of the silent era alongside D.W. Griffith and Cecil B. DeMille, which certainly fits Stroheim. A clip of his troubled epic *Queen Kelly* (1929), produced by and starring Swanson, even makes an appearance in *Sunset Boulevard*, which became the first time any part of that silent film was seen by audiences. And of course DeMille had played a major role in Gloria's life and career. The six movies they made together, starting when she was only a teen, turned her into an international superstar.

DeMille once called Swanson the "movie star of all movie stars," and Wilder has Stroheim's character Max remind the audience that Norma "was the greatest star of them all." Gloria earned recognition as the first clotheshorse in Hollywood, known for her high style on-screen as well as off. Her films with DeMille, such as *Why Change Your Wife?* (1920), were known for the quality and quantity of the star's costumes. In fact, DeMille found fashion to be an integral part of the Swanson formula for success: "sex, sets, and costumes."

During those years, costume designers Clare West, Ethel Chaffin, and Mitchell Leisen dressed her in styles ranging from European couture to their own custom-made clothes. They draped luxurious fabrics loosely on Swanson's petite figure, and accents like beading and feathers made her an Art Deco goddess. Audiences lined up again and again for her "fashion films" (as DeMille called them), and everyone wanted to be as glamorous as Gloria. She wielded such influence that she shaped much of early 1920s style.

Edith Head relished the opportunity to work with her idol, Gloria Swanson. (Everett Collection)

Swanson reigned in the first half of the decade as queen of the movies, but in 1925 she flew to France and married Marquis Henri de la Falaise de Coudray. Global fanfare surrounded the marriage, including parades in both New York and Los Angeles. Upon Gloria's return to Paramount, she passed through the gates in what Romans would call a triumph—the entire studio lined the streets and threw roses at the procession and then at her feet when

Swanson emerged from her Rolls-Royce. The event became enough of Hollywood legend that Wilder references it in *Sunset Boulevard* when William Holden as Joe Gillis describes Norma as a former star "still waving proudly to a parade that had long since passed her by."

Costume designer Edith Head was among the adoring employees who lined up to greet Swanson with petals in hand. Head never forgot the experience. "In my mind, Gloria represented the greatest from the days when I was just a beginner," Head would remember. "She was a legend when I was walking around with stars in my eyes."

Two years before Swanson's return, Edith had started at Paramount as a sketch artist and assistant to head costume designer Howard Greer. For fifteen years she had learned everything there was to know about costume design from the creators of "Paramount Polish." Greer and Travis Banton had taught her about fabrics, design techniques, and the production process. She had turned out to be a natural and complemented the genius twosome with her gift for management and politics. When Head started, Swanson was at her height of popularity and worked only with the best, which meant Banton and Greer. Edith's tasks included washing Gloria's hosiery.

As pre-production of *Sunset Boulevard* began, Head relished the opportunity to design for Gloria. "Dressing her meant dressing an idol," she remembered. Though at first she was anxious about working with a "meticulous" ac-

Many of Gloria's costumes drew on her early 1920s style. (Top photo, GKB Collection; bottom photo, Everett Collection)

tress so well versed in fashion—both Banton and Greer had spoken of Swanson's exacting nature—Edith found she already had an admirer in Gloria. After all, Head had enjoyed great success since succeeding Banton as Paramount's head of costume design in 1938, including contributing to style in influential film noir. She had created the costumes for Barbara Stanwyck in *Double Indemnity* and *The Strange Love of Martha Ivers*. She had also helped create Veronica Lake's look in *This Gun for Hire*, *The Glass Key*, and *The Blue Dahlia*. Now she would help create even more groundbreaking film noir style for Gloria in *Sunset Boulevard*.

From the beginning of production, everyone was clear about the character of Norma Desmond. Billy Wilder remembered Head saying, "Although her greatest moments were in her silent movie days, Norma Desmond tried to be as contemporary as possible by wearing fashionable styles, clothes, and makeup; yet there was something about her that connoted a sense of the past, a bit of dèjá vu."

Norma's New Year's Eve party gown mixes the exotic flair of the 1920s with a voluminous 1950s silhouette. (Everett Collection)

For Edith, this translated into merging the styles of the New Look with those of the Jazz Age. The waists of the costumes were generally nipped in to be current with 1950s style, but she also incorporated some looser silhouettes of the 1920s as well. Norma is bigger than life, so Head used tricks with those silhouettes to elongate the five-foot-tall Swanson on-screen. One example is her long-sleeved, floor-length lounging gown, which features similarities to dresses Head had created for the equally petite Veronica Lake. She also relies on heavy accents of fur and even peacock feathers that were popular in the earlier era. The extensive use of fur—a mink-lined cape with a matching spiral mink hat, a chinchilla wrap over a brocade dress, and a cape lined in ermine accessorized with an ermine cuff muff—signifies Norma Desmond's predatory nature.

In addition, leopard appears in the look of Norma's swimming pool ensemble and even in the upholstery of her car. The final details are in the avalanche of accessories, layers of oversized jewelry, and the famous cigarette holder that pushes every look over the top.

Everything was pitch perfect because Head had the ultimate resource in her style-setting star. Swanson advised her in clothes, hair, and makeup, but also made sure to describe how actors moved on-screen in the age of the silents. Gloria used those melo-dramatic gestures in the film to bring out the character, and Edith said she "added a touch of the bizarre to each costume to remind audiences that [Norma] was living in a dream world of the past." This proved especially true in the final scene when the character re-gresses to the early days of silent cinema. Her costume reflects Gloria's own less-structured and over-accessorized exotic early 1920s style. That said, Head knew there were limits; Wilder was firm in his direction that he didn't want anything ridiculous or laughable. Thus,

The fur and animal print in *Sunset Boulevard*, from the costumes to the car upholstery, signify Norma Desmond's predatory nature. (Top photo, Everett Collection; bottom photo, GKB Collection)

Norma is seen in fashionable styles, yet her complicated clothes contrast with the wardrobe of other characters, such as young Betty Schaefer (Nancy Olson). Betty wears simple suits, sweaters, and skirts with very little jewelry.

William Holden's costumes are equally telling about his character, Joe Gillis. Early in the film, the unemployed screenwriter lives in a sports jacket and baggy trousers. Eventually, Norma's complaints about his clothes prompt a trip to the best tailor in Hollywood and a new wardrobe: eighteen custom-made suits, six dozen shirts, and a vicuna overcoat that feels like mink. His closet even includes a tuxedo with tails, a style so clearly outdated that his friend jokingly compares him to Adolphe Menjou. Accessories become an important part of Joe's new look—custom-made shoes along with a watch, cuff links, platinum key chain, and gold cigarette case engraved with "Mad about the boy" (referenced in 2006's *Hollywoodland*). In the end as Joe tries to reclaim his life, he rejects everything Desmond bought and slides back into his old ill-fitting jacket and pants to say goodbye.

In the end Norma regresses to her years as a silent star. The costume reflects some of Swanson's signature style at the height of her popularity. (Everett Collection)

Despite Head's meticulous attention to detail in the costume design for *Sunset Boulevard*, her work failed to earn an Academy Award nomination in 1950. Even so, Head would win two of her eight Oscars that year. She earned one for dressing Bette Davis in the black-and-white *All About Eve* and another as part of the design team for DeMille's color epic, *Samson and Delilah*. Coincidentally, this is the very film DeMille is directing in his scenes for *Sunset Boulevard*.

Even without an official accolade, Edith took great pride in her work for *Sunset Boulevard*. It was the opportunity to succeed her mentors and dress her idol, transforming the already glamorous Gloria Swanson into the tragic and unforgettable Norma Desmond.

Above: Norma's suicide attempt prompts Joe Gillis to turn in his tuxedo, vicuna coat, and the rest of his new wardrobe. Below: Many of Edith Head's costumes in *Sunset Boulevard* say goodbye to 1940s style, including this memorable scene where Norma acknowledges the end of the silent era. (Both photos, Everett Collection)

Chapter Notes

From Depression to War

Amadeo, Kimberly. "Unemployment Rate by Year Since 1929 Compared to Inflation and GDP." The Balance. 3 January 2020. Accessed online https://www.thebalance.com/unemployment-rate-by-year-3305506 4 January 2020.

Bond, David. *The Guinness Guide to 20th Century Fashion*. Enfield, Middlesex: Guinness Publishing, 1981.

King, Susan. "How Did Wizard of Oz Fare on its 1939 Release?" *Los Angeles Times*. 11 March 2013. Accessed online 3 January 2020 https://www.latimes.com/entertainment/movies/la-xpm-2013-mar-11-la-et-mn-original-wizard-reaction-20130311-story.html.

Koerner, Katherine. "Op-ed: The Cost of a Movie, from the Great Depression to the Great Recession." *Seattle Times*. 14 December 2012. Accessed online 3 January 2020 https://www.seattletimes.com/opinion/op-ed-the-cost-of-a-movie-from-the-great-depression-to-the-great-recession/

"Labor Force, Employment, and Unemployment, 1929-39: Estimating Methods." Bureau of Labor Statistics. Page 2, Table 1. Accessed online 3 January 2020 https://www.bls.gov/opub/mlr/1948/article/pdf/labor-force-employment-and-unemployment-1929-39-estimating-methods.pdf

Pautz, Michelle. "The Decline in Average Weekly Cinema Attendance: 1930-2000." Issues in Political Economy. Vol. 11. 2002. Accessed online http://org.elon.edu/ipe/pautz2.pdf 4 January 2020.

Sickels, Robert. *The 1940s*. Westport: Greenwood Press, 2004.

Taylor, Kerry. *Vintage Fashion and Couture: From Poiret to McQueen*. Buffalo, NY: Firefly Books, 2013.

Uschan, Michael V. *The 1940s: A Cultural History of the United States Through the Decades*. San Diego: Lucent Books, 1999.

Walford, Jonathan. *Forties Fashion: From Siren Suits to the New Look*. New York: Thames & Hudson, 2008.

Winkler, Allan M. *Home Front U.S.A.: America During World War II*. Wheeling, WV: Harlan Davidson, 2012.

The Maltese Falcon

Benchley, Nathaniel. *Humphrey Bogart*. Boston: Little, Brown and Company, 1975.

Bogart, Stephen. *Bogart: In Search of My Father*. New York: Dutton, 1995.

Grobel, Lawrence. *The Hustons*. New York: Charles Scribner's Sons, 1989.

Hammett, Dashiell. *Dashiell Hammett: Five Complete Novels*. New York: Avenel Books, 1986.

Huston, John. *An Open Book*. New York: Alfred A Knopf, 1980.

Hyams, Joe. *Bogart & Bacall: A Love Story*. New York: David McKay Company, 1975.

Kanfer, Stefan. *Tough Without a Gun: The Life and Extraordinary Afterlife of Humphrey Bogart*. New York: Alfred A. Knopf, 2011.

Muller, Eddie. *Dark City: The Lost World of Film Noir*. New York: St. Martin's Griffin, 1998.

Muller, Eddie. The Maltese Falcon. Introduction to Noir Alley. Accessed online on YouTube https:// www.youtube.com/watch?v=AeDZDzXkJ2k 28 September 2019.

Orry-Kelly. *Women I've Undressed: The Fabulous Life and Times of a Legendary Hollywood Designer*. London: Allen & Unwin, 2016.

Schatz, Thomas. *Boom and Bust: American Cinema in the 1940s*. Berkeley: University of California Press, 1997.

Sperber, A.M. and Eric Lax. *Bogart*. New York: HarperCollins, 1997.

Wilde, Meta Carpenter and Orin Borsten. *A Loving Gentleman: The Love Story of William Faulkner and Meta Carpenter*. New York: Simon and Schuster, 1976.

I Wake Up Screaming

"All-American Sextet of Best Dressed Film Stars." *The Scranton Times*. 22 November 1933. 8. Accessed Newspapers.com 23 Dec 2019.

"Another Film Figure Wins Title." *Oakland Tribune*. 28 July 1940. 71. Accessed Newspapers.com 20 Dec 2019.

Coons, Robbin. "Betty Grable Planned She'd Quit Films, Take Life Easy." *The Bergen Evening Record*. 16 August 1940. 10. Accessed Newspapers.com 20 Dec 2019.

Flagg, James Montgomery. "Mr. Flagg in Hollywood: Carole Landis is No 'Wudgie-Wudgie.'" *The Boston Globe*. 7 November 1941. 15. Accessed Newspapers.com 23 Dec 2019.

Friedrich, Otto. *City of Nets: A Portrait of Hollywood in the 1940s*. New York: Harper Perennial, 1980.

"Fugitive From a Leg Art Career: Or is She?" *Minneapolis Star Journal*. 27 May 1940. 21. Accessed Newspapers.com 20 Dec 2019.

Gans, Eric. *Carole Landis: A Most Beautiful Girl*. Jackson, MS: University Press of Mississippi, 2008.

"Gwen Wakeling Costume Design Drawings." Margaret Herrick Library. AMPAS. Online. Accessed https://collections.oscars.org/link/bio/351 23 Dec 2019.

Jorgensen, Jay and Donald L. Scoggins. *Creating the Illusion: A Fashionable History of Hollywood Costume Designers*. Philadelphia: Running Press, 2015.

"Leader in Design." *The Evening Independent*. 11 March 1936. 12. Accessed Newspapers.com 23 Dec 2019.

McClelland, Doug. *Forties Film Talk: Oral Histories of Hollywood*. Jefferson: McFarland & Company, 1992.

Muller, Eddie. *Dark City: The Lost World of Film Noir*. New York: St. Martin's Griffin, 1998.

Muller, Eddie. *I Wake Up Screaming*. DVD audio commentary. 20th Century Fox, 2006.

Silver, Alain and Elizabeth Ward, eds. *Film Noir: An Encyclopedic Reference to the American Style*. New York: The Overlook Press, 1980.

"'Ping Girl' Title Flatly Disdained by Carole Landis, Paid Ads Reveal." *The Rock Island Argus*. 27 May 1940. 20. Accessed Newspapers.com 23 Dec 2019.

The Shanghai Gesture

Baxter, John. *The Cinema of Josef von Sternberg*. New York: A.S. Barnes & Co., 1971.

Cassini, Oleg. *In My Own Fashion: An Autobiography*. New York: Simon and Schuster, 1987.

The Des Moines Register. 1 February 1942. 6. Accessed Newspapers.com 19 November 2019.

"'Doesn't Understand.'" *The New York Daily News*. 14 September 1941. 23C. Accessed Newspapers.com 19 November 2019.

"Gene Tierney Displays Latest Fashion Creations." *The Ottawa Journal*. 7 March 1942. 15, Accessed Newspapers.com 19 November 2019.

Jorgensen, Jay and Donald L. Scoggins. *Creating the Illusion: A Fashionable History of Hollywood Costume Designers*. Philadelphia: Running Press, 2015.

Othman, Frederick C. "Star's Titled Gown Designer-Husband Has Ideas." *Rochester Democrat and Chronicle*. 21 December 1941. 8D. Accessed Newspapers.com 19 November 2019.

Patrick, Corbin. "An Oriental Drama." *The Indianapolis Star*. 5 March 1942. 14. Accessed Newspapers.com 19 November 2019.

Pollock, Arthur. "Shanghai Gesture is Finally Filmed and Sent to Astor." *The Brooklyn Daily Eagle*. 26 December 1941. 11. Accessed Newspapers.com 19 November 2019.

Riva, Maria. *Marlene Dietrich*. New York: Alfred A. Knopf, 1993.

Schatz, Thomas. *Boom and Bust: American Cinema in the 1940s*. Berkeley: University of California Press, 1997.

Scheibel, Will. "Working It: Gene Tierney, Laura, and Wartime Beautification." *Camera Obscura*. Vol. 33, Number 2 (98). 1 September 2018. 161-195. Downloaded from Duke University Press 9 November 2019.

"The Shanghai Gesture, Fascinating Mystery." *Valley Sunday Star-Monitor-Herald*. 3 May 1942. 14.

Accessed Newspapers.com 19 November 2019.

"The Shanghai Gesture Now at Elgin Theatre." *The Ottawa Journal.* 28 February 1942. 26. Accessed Newspapers.com 19 November 2019.

"The Shanghai Gesture Unfolds Stirring Drama." *The Morning Herald.* 2 March 1942. 4. Accessed Newspapers.com 19 November 2019.

Tierney, Gene. *Self-Portrait.* New York: Wyden Books, 1978.

Vogel, Michelle. *Gene Tierney: A Biography.* Jefferson: McFarland & Company, Inc., 2005.

Weinberg, Herman G. *Josef von Sternberg: A Critical Study of the Great Film Director.* New York: E.P. Dutton & Co., 1967.

Patriotic Style

Amadeo, Kimberly. "Unemployment Rate by Year Since 1929 Compared to Inflation and GDP." The Balance. 3 January 2020. Accessed online https://www.thebalance.com/unemployment-rate-by-year-3305506 4 January 2020.

Bond, David. *The Guinness Guide to 20th Century Fashion.* Enfield, Middlesex: Guinness Publishing, 1981.

Haver, Ronald. David O. Selznick's Hollywood. New York: *Bonanza Books*, 1980.

Head, Edith and Paddy Calistro. *Edith Head's Hollywood.* Santa Monica: Angel City Press, 2008.

Jorgensen, Jay. *Edith Head: The 50-Year Career of Hollywood's Greatest Costume Designer.* Philadelphia: Running Press, 2010.

King, Susan. "How Did Wizard of Oz Fare on its 1939 Release?" *Los Angeles Times.* 11 March 2013. Accessed online 3 January 2020 https://www.latimes.com/entertainment/movies/la-xpm-2013-mar-11-la-et-mn-original-wizard-reaction-20130311-story.html

Koerner, Katherine. "Op-ed: The Cost of a Movie, from the Great Depression to the Great Recession." *Seattle Times.* 14 December 2012. Accessed online 3 January 2020 https://www.seattletimes.com/opinion/op-ed-the-cost-of-a-movie-from-the-great-depression-to-the-great-recession/

"Labor Force, Employment, and Unemployment, 1929-39: Estimating Methods." Bureau of Labor Statistics. Page 2, Table 1. Accessed online 3 January 2020 https://www.bls.gov/opub/mlr/1948/article/pdf/labor-force-employment-and-unemployment-1929-39-estimating-methods.pdf

Pautz, Michelle. "The Decline in Average Weekly Cinema Attendance: 1930-2000." Issues in Political Economy. Vol. 11. 2002. Accessed online http://org.elon.edu/ipe/pautz2.pdf 4 January 2020.

"US Military by the Numbers." The National WWII Museum. Accessed online https://www.nationalww2museum.org/students-teachers/student-resources/research-starters/research-starters-us-military-numbers 9 January 2020.

Schatz, Thomas. *Boom and Bust: American Cinema in the 1940s.* Berkeley: University of California Press, 1997.

Sickels, Robert. *The 1940s.* Westport: Greenwood Press, 2004.

Taylor, Kerry. *Vintage Fashion and Couture: From Poiret to McQueen.* Buffalo, NY: Firefly Books,

2013.

Uschan, Michael V. *The 1940s: A Cultural History of the United States Through the Decades*. San Diego: Lucent Books, 1999.

"Veronica Lake's Hair." *LIFE*. 24 November 1941. 59-61. Accessed online 9 Jan 2020 https://books.google.com/books?id=UU4EAAAAMBAJ&lpg=PA58&dq=life%20veronica%20lake's%20hair&pg=PA59#v=onepage&q=Miss%20Lake's%20head%20of%20hair&f=false

Walford, Jonathan. *Forties Fashion: From Siren Suits to the New Look*. New York: Thames & Hudson, 2008.

Winkler, Allan M. *Home Front U.S.A.: America During World War II*. Wheeling, WV: Harlan Davidson, 2012.

This Gun for Hire

Brownmiller, Susan. *Femininity*. New York: Fawcett Columbine, 1984.

"Cinema Chatter." *Harrisburg Sunday Courier*. 14 June 1942: 4. Print. Accessed at Newspapers.com 13 August 2019.

Greer, Howard. *Designing Male*. New York: G.P. Putnam's Sons, 1951.

Harrison, Paul. "Hollywood Happenings." *The Tampa Times*. 23 May 1942: 14. Accessed at Newspapers.com 13 August 2019.

Head, Edith and Paddy Calistro. *Edith Head's Hollywood*. Santa Monica: Angel City Press, 2008.

Hogan, David J. *Film Noir FAQ*. Milwaukee: Applause Theatre & Cinema Books, 2013.

Jorgensen, Jay and Donald L. Scoggins. *Creating the Illusion: A Fashionable History of Hollywood Costume Designers*. Philadelphia: Running Press, 2015.

Jorgensen, Jay. *Edith Head: The 50-Year Career of Hollywood's Greatest Costume Designer*. Philadelphia: Running Press, 2010.

McKay, Margaret. "Fashion Scene." *The San Bernardino County Sun*. 11 January 1942:16. Print. Accessed at Newspapers.com 13 August 2019.

"Meyer Regenstein Purchases Lock of Veronica Lake's Hair." *The Atlanta Constitution*. 30 September 1942: 1. Print. Accessed at Newspapers.com 13 August 2019.

Muller, Eddie (TCM host and film noir expert). Interview by author, 13 April 2012.

"New Button Style." *The Bergen Evening Record*. 31 March 1942: 12. Print. Accessed at Newspapers.com 13 August 2019.

Peak, Mayme Ober. "I Cover Hollywood: Veronica Lake a Rare Specimen." *The Boston Daily Globe*. 6 April 1942: 6. Print. Accessed at Newspapers.com 13 August 2019.

Osborne, Robert (host of Turner Classic Movies). Interview by author, 12 April 2012.

"Safety Styles." U.S. News Review. YouTube video. 1:45 1940s Glamour Girl. 8 August 2013. https://www.youtube.com/watch?v=80LFNFhcSPM

Schatz, Thomas. *Boom and Bust: American Cinema in the 1940s*. Berkeley: University of California

Press, 1997.

"Stars of Motion Picture Attractions at Moline Theaters." *The Daily Dispatch Moline Illinois.* 24 October 1942: 8. Print. Accessed at Newspapers.com 13 August 2019.

Thropp, Randall (Paramount costume archivist). Interview by author, 13 August 2019.

Double Indemnity

Cain, James M. *The Postman Always Rings Twice, Double Indemnity, Mildred Pierce, and Selected Stories.* New York: Alfred A. Knopf, 2003.

Head, Edith and Paddy Calistro. *Edith Head's Hollywood.* Santa Monica: Angel City Press, 2008.

Hogan, David J. *Film Noir FAQ.* Milwaukee: Applause Theatre & Cinema Books, 2013.

Hopper, Hedda. "No Dice." *The Harrisburg Telegraph.* 11 October 1943. 17.

Jorgensen, Jay and Donald L. Scoggins. *Creating the Illusion: A Fashionable History of Hollywood Costume Designers.* Philadelphia: Running Press, 2015.

Jorgensen, Jay. *Edith Head: The 50-Year Career of Hollywood's Greatest Costume Designer.* Philadelphia: Running Press, 2010.

Joseff, Kristin (family member of Eugene Joseff and current head of Joseff of Hollywood). Correspondence with author, 26 August 2019.

Kobal, John. *People Will Talk.* New York: Alfred A. Knopf, 1986.

Lally, Kevin. *Wilder Times: The Life of Billy Wilder.* New York: Henry Holt and Company, 1996.

Muller, Eddie. *Dark City: The Lost World of Film Noir.* New York: St. Martin's Press, 1998.

Osborne, Robert. *Introduction to Double Indemnity.* DVD.

Phillips, Gene D. *Some Like It Wilder: The Life and Controversial Films of Billy Wilder.* Lexington, KY: The University Press of Kentucky, 2010.

Polito, Robert. *Introduction to The Postman Always Rings Twice, Double Indemnity, Mildred Pierce, and Selected Stories*, ix–xxiv. New York: Alfred A. Knopf, 2003.

Schatz, Thomas. *Boom and Bust: American Cinema in the 1940s.* Berkeley: University of California Press, 1997.

Thropp, Randall (Paramount costume archivist). Interview by author, 13 August 2019.

Vieira, Mark A. *Into the Dark: The Hidden World of Film Noir*, 1941-1950. Philadelphia: Running Press, 2016.

Wilder, Billy and Raymond Chandler. *Double Indemnity.* Film script. 27 November 1943. Accessed 20 August 2019 http://www.public.asu.edu/~srbeatty/394/Double%20Indemnity.pdf

Wilson, Victoria. *A Life of Barbara Stanwyck: Steel-True 1907-1940.* New York: Simon & Schuster, 2013.

Laura

"Bonnie Cashin; Influential Fashion Designer." *Los Angeles Times.* 6 February 2000. B10. Accessed

Newspapers.com 9 November 2019.

Christy, Marian. "After a Fashion: Cashin the Independent." *The Arizona Republic*. 2 July 1969. 16. Accessed Newspapers.com 9 November 2019.

Christy, Marian. "After a Fashion: Designer Thinks Indian." *Quad-City Times*. 15 February 1971. 11. Accessed Newspapers.com 9 November 2019.

Heaton, Ray. "SSO Schedules Mystery-Romance for Sunday Movie." *Hawaii Tribune-Herald*. 14 April 1945. 3. Accessed Newspapers.com 9 November 2019.

Hogan, David J. *Film Noir FAQ*. Milwaukee: Applause Theatre & Cinema Books, 2013.

Jorgensen, Jay and Donald L. *Scoggins. Creating the Illusion: A Fashionable History of Hollywood Costume Designers*. Philadelphia: Running Press, 2015.

Kirkham, Pat. *Women Designers in the U.S.A. 1900-2000*. New Haven: Yale University Press, 2000.

Martin, Mildred. "Honey of a Homicidal Yarn Enlivens Screen in 'Laura.'" *The Philadelphia Inquirer*. 12 November 1944. 14. Accessed Newspapers.com 9 November 2019.

McClelland, Doug. *Forties Film Talk: Oral Histories of Hollywood*. Jefferson: McFarland & Company, 1992.

Muller, Eddie. *Dark City: The Lost World of Film Noir*. New York: St. Martin's Press, 1998.

Murphy, Robert E. "'Laura' in Group of Fine Mysteries." *Minneapolis Sunday Tribune*. 29 October 1944. 8. Accessed Newspapers.com 9 November 2019.

Schatz, Thomas. *Boom and Bust: American Cinema in the 1940s*. Berkeley: University of California Press, 1997.

Scheibel, Will. "Working It: Gene Tierney, Laura, and Wartime Beautification." *Camera Obscura*. Vol. 33, Number 2 (98). 1 September 2018. 161-195. Downloaded from Duke University Press 9 November 2019.

Vieira, Mark A. *Into the Dark: The Hidden World of Film Noir*, 1941-1950. Philadelphia: Running Press, 2016.

Vogel, Michelle. *Gene Tierney: A Biography*. Jefferson: McFarland & Company, 2005.

To Have and Have Not

Bacall, Lauren. *By Myself*. New York: Alfred A. Knopf, 1979.

Benchley, Nathaniel. *Humphrey Bogart*. Boston: Little, Brown and Company, 1975.

Bogart, Stephen. *Bogart: In Search of My Father*. New York: Dutton, 1995.

Hyams, Joe. *Bogart & Bacall: A Love Story*. New York: David McKay Company, 1975.

Kanfer, Stefan. *Tough Without a Gun: The Life and Extraordinary Afterlife of Humphrey Bogart*. New York: Alfred A. Knopf, 2011.

Kobal, John. *People Will Talk*. New York: Alfred A. Knopf, 1986.

McCarthy, Todd. *Howard Hawks: The Grey Fox of Hollywood*. New York: Grove Press, 1997.

Parish, James Robert and Don E. Stanke. *The Forties Gals*. Westport, CT: Arlington, 1980.

Quirk, Lawrence J. *Lauren Bacall: Her Films and Career.* New Jersey: The Citadel Press, 1986.

Schatz, Thomas. *Boom and Bust: American Cinema in the 1940s.* Berkeley: University of California Press, 1997.

Sperber, A.M. and Eric Lax. *Bogart.* New York: HarperCollins, 1997.

Taylor, Kerry. *Vintage Fashion and Couture: From Poiret to McQueen.* Buffalo, NY: Firefly Books, 2013.

Murder, My Sweet

Chandler, Raymond. *Farewell, My Lovely.* New York: Random House, 1940.

Dmytryk, Edward and Jean Patrick Dmytryk. *Hollywood's Golden Age: As Told By One Who Lived It All.* Albany, NY: BearManor Media, 2003.

Hart, Alicia. "Glorifying Yourself: Jewelry Needs Plain Background." *The Fresno Bee.* 7 July 1945. 5. Accessed at Newspapers.com 25 October 2019.

Hogan, David J. *Film Noir FAQ.* Milwaukee: Applause Theatre & Cinema Books, 2013.

Jorgensen, Jay and Donald L. Scoggins. *Creating the Illusion: A Fashionable History of Hollywood Costume Designers.* Philadelphia: Running Press, 2015.

Krug, Karl. "The Man Who Came Back." *Pittsburgh Sun-Telegraph.* 27 January 1946. Section 2 page 6. Accessed at Newspapers.com 26 October 2019.

McLellan, Dennis. "The 'New' Dick Powell." *Los Angeles Times.* 17 September 1998. 14R. Accessed at Newspapers.com 26 October 2019.

Muller, Eddie. *Dark City: The Lost World of Film Noir.* New York: St. Martin's Press, 1998.

Schatz, Thomas. *Boom and Bust: American Cinema in the 1940s.* Berkeley: University of California Press, 1997.

Scheuer, Philip K. "Fates Still Fickle to Claire Trevor." *Los Angeles Times.* 12 August 1945. Part III, 1 and 3. Accessed at Newspapers.com 25 October 2019.

Scott, Vernon. "Watch Out Presley—Dick Powell Sings Again." *Nevada Sate Journal.* 26 November 1957. 4. Accessed at Newspapers.com 26 October 2019.

"Short Cut Led Trevor to Screen." *The Hartford Courant.* 6 August 1939. A1. Accessed at Newspapers.com 25 October 2019.

Vieira, Mark A. *Into the Dark: The Hidden World of Film Noir, 1941-1950.* Philadelphia: Running Press, 2016.

Whittemore, Hank. "My Life in Hollywood's Golden Age." *The Lincoln Star, Parade Magazine.* 20 February 1994. 14-15. Accessed at Newspapers.com 25 October 2019.

Mildred Pierce

Cain, James M. *The Postman Always Rings Twice, Double Indemnity, Mildred Pierce, and Selected Stories.* New York: Alfred A. Knopf, 2003.

Carroll, Harrison. "Hollywood Behind the Scenes." *The Press Democrat.* 21 January 1945. 1. Accessed Newspapers.com 1 November 2019.

Chandler, Charlotte. *Not the Girl Next Door*. New York: Simon & Schuster, 2008.

Chierichetti, David. "Milo Anderson: Quiet Man with Resounding Talent for Costumes." *Los Angeles Times*. 19 August 1983. V: 1, 18, 22. Accessed Newspapers.com 1 November 2019.

Heffernan, Harold. "Hollywood to Battle Paris as Style Center." *The Miami Daily News*. 11 March 1945. 4-C. Accessed Newspapers.com 1 November 2019.

Hogan, David J. *Film Noir FAQ*. Milwaukee: Applause Theatre & Cinema Books, 2013.

"Joan Crawford, Milland Win Hollywood 'Oscars.'" *The Salinas Californian*. 8 March 1946. 1. Accessed Newspapers.com 1 November 2109.

Jorgensen, Jay and Donald Scoggins. *Creating the Illusion: A Fashionable History of Hollywood Costume Designers*. Philadelphia: Running Press, 2015.

Kobal, John. *People Will Talk*. New York: Alfred A. Knopf, 1986.

McClelland, Doug. *Forties Film Talk: Oral Histories of Hollywood*. Jefferson: McFarland & Company, 1992.

Muller, Eddie. *Dark City: The Lost World of Film Noir*. New York: St. Martin's Press, 1998.

Quirk, Lawrence J. and William Schoell. *Joan Crawford: The Essential Biography*. Lexington, KY: The University Press of Kentucky, 2002.

Rode, Alan K. *Michael Curtiz: A Life in Film*. Lexington: University Press of Kentucky, 2017.

Schatz, Thomas. *Boom and Bust: American Cinema in the 1940s*. Berkeley: University of California Press, 1997.

Spoto, Donald. *Possessed: The Life of Joan Crawford*. New York: HarperCollins, 2010.

Homecoming

Amadeo, Kimberly. "Unemployment Rate by Year Since 1929 Compared to Inflation and GDP." The Balance. 3 January 2020. Accessed online https://www.thebalance.com/unemployment-rate-by-year-3305506 4 January 2020.

Bond, David. *The Guinness Guide to 20th Century Fashion*. Enfield, Middlesex: Guinness Publishing, 1981.

Haver, Ronald. *David O. Selznick's Hollywood*. New York: Bonanza Books, 1980.

Head, Edith and Paddy Calistro. *Edith Head's Hollywood*. Santa Monica: Angel City Press, 2008.

Jorgensen, Jay. *Edith Head: The 50-Year Career of Hollywood's Greatest Costume Designer*. Philadelphia: Running Press, 2010.

King, Susan. "How Did Wizard of Oz Fare on its 1939 Release?" *Los Angeles Times*. 11 March 2013. Accessed online 3 January 2020 https://www.latimes.com/entertainment/movies/la-xpm-2013-mar-11-la-et-mn-original-wizard-reaction-20130311-story.html

Koerner, Katherine. "Op-ed: The Cost of a Movie, from the Great Depression to the Great Recession." *Seattle Times*. 14 December 2012. Accessed online 3 January 2020 https://www.seattletimes.

com/opinion/op-ed-the-cost-of-a-movie-from-the-great-depression-to-the-great-recession/

"Labor Force, Employment, and Unemployment, 1929-39: Estimating Methods." Bureau of Labor Statistics. Page 2, Table 1. Accessed online 3 January 2020 https://www.bls.gov/opub/mlr/1948/article/pdf/labor-force-employment-and-unemployment-1929-39-estimating-methods.pdf

Marshman, Donald. "Mister SEE'-ODD-MAK." *LIFE*. 25 August 1947. 101. Accessed online 9 January 2020 https://books.google.com/books?id=LUIEAAAAMBAJ&lpg=PA100&pg=PA100#v=onepage&q&f=false

Pautz, Michelle. "The Decline in Average Weekly Cinema Attendance: 1930-2000." Issues in Political Economy. Vol. 11. 2002. Accessed online http://org.elon.edu/ipe/pautz2.pdf 4 January 2020.

Schatz, Thomas. *Boom and Bust: American Cinema in the 1940s*. Berkeley: University of California Press, 1997.

Sickels, Robert. *The 1940s*. Westport: Greenwood Press, 2004.

Taylor, Kerry. *Vintage Fashion and Couture: From Poiret to McQueen*. Buffalo, NY: Firefly Books, 2013.

Uschan, Michael V. *The 1940s: A Cultural History of the United States Through the Decades*. San Diego: Lucent Books, 1999.

Walford, Jonathan. *Forties Fashion: From Siren Suits to the New Look*. New York: Thames & Hudson, 2008.

Winkler, Allan M. *Home Front U.S.A.: America During World War II*. Wheeling, WV: Harlan Davidson, 2012.

Gilda

"Costume in The Metropolitan Museum of Art." September 2014. Online. Accessed https://www.metmuseum.org/toah/hd/cost/hd_cost.htm 27 July 2019.

Gliatto, Tom, Anne Marie Otey, Ulrica Wihlborg, and Nancy Matsumoto. "The Gift of Garb." *People*. 12 May 1997: 44-45. Print. Accessed at Margaret Herrick Library (AMPAS) 16 April 2015.

Jackson, Beverly. *Santa Barbara News Press*. 7 October 1990. Accessed at Margaret Herrick Library (AMPAS) 16 April 2005.

"Jean Louis." *People*. 9 February 1987: 76. Print. Accessed at Margaret Herrick Library (AMPAS) 16 April 2015.

"Jean Louis." *The Times* (London). 26 April 1997: unknown. Print. Accessed at Margaret Herrick Library (AMPAS) 16 April 2015.

"Jean Louis and His First Ladies." *W*. 27 March 1981: unknown. Print. Accessed at Margaret Herrick Library (AMPAS) 16 April 2015.

Jorgensen, Jay and Donald L. Scoggins. *Creating the Illusion: A Fashionable History of Hollywood Costume Designers*. Philadelphia: Running Press, 2015.

Kobal, John. *People Will Talk*. New York: Alfred A. Knopf, 1986.

Leaming, Barbara. *If This Was Happiness: A Biography of Rita Hayworth*. New York: Viking Penguin,

1989.

Louis, Jean. Publicity interview on his career. Hollywood: Columbia Pictures, 20 July 1954. Print. Accessed at Margaret Herrick Library (AMPAS) 16 April 2015.

Modern Screen. January-June 1946. 8. Print. Accessed at Margaret Herrick Library (AMPAS) 16 April 2015.

Neophytou, Nadia. "The Met's Costume Institute to Showcase Collection of Film Buff Fashion Historian." *The Hollywood Reporter*. 26 July 2019. Online. Accessed https://www.hollywoodreporter.com/news/met-s-costume-institute-showcase-fashion-historian-sandy-schreiers-collection-1226600 27 July 2019.

Sanders, James R. "Rita Hayworth." *Vogue Italia*. 9 August 2012. Online. Accessed https://www.vogue.it/en/vogue-curvy/glam-and-curvy/2012/08/rita-hayworth 27 July 2019.

Stack, Rosemarie. "Natural Elegance." *Movieline*. 25 July 1986: unknown. Accessed at Margaret Herrick Library (AMPAS) 16 April 2015.

Vallance, Tom. "Obituary: Jean Louis." *The Independent*. 25 April 1997. Online. Accessed https://www.independent.co.uk/news/obituaries/obituary-jean-louis-1269135.html 27 July 2019.

The Postman Always Rings Twice

Billecci, Frank and Lauranne B. Fisher. *Irene A Designer from the Golden Age of Hollywood: The MGM Years 1942-1949*. Atglen, PA: Schiffer Publishing, 2013.

Cane, James M. *The Postman Always Rings Twice, Double Indemnity, Mildred Pierce, and Selected Stories*. New York: Alfred A. Knopf, 2003.

Crane, Cheryl. *Detour: A Hollywood Story*. New York: Arbor House. 1988.

Film Noir: 75 Years of the Greatest Crime Films. *LIFE*, August 19, 2016.

Jorgensen, Jay and Donald L. Scoggins. *Creating the Illusion: A Fashionable History of Hollywood Costume Designers*. Philadelphia: Running Press, 2015.

Morella, Joe and Edward Z. Epstein. *Lana: The Public and Private Lives of Miss Turner*. New York: Citadel Press, 1971.

Notorious

Haver, Ronald. *David O. Selznick's Hollywood*. New York: Bonanza Books, 1980.

Head, Edith and Paddy Calistro. *Edith Head's Hollywood*. Santa Monica: Angel City Press, 2008.

Hogan, David J. *Film Noir FAQ*. Milwaukee: Applause Theatre & Cinema Books, 2013.

Jorgensen, Jay and Donald L. Scoggins. *Creating the Illusion: A Fashionable History of Hollywood Costume Designers*. Philadelphia: Running Press, 2015.

Jorgensen, Jay. *Edith Head: The 50-Year Career of Hollywood's Greatest Costume Designer*. Philadelphia: Running Press, 2010.

Kobal, John. *People Will Talk*. New York: Alfred A. Knopf, 1986.

Maslin, Janet. "Ingrid Bergman and the Enduring Appeal of Notorious." *The New York Times*. 26 October 1980. Accessed online https://archive.nytimes.com/www.nytimes.com/library/ film/102680 hitch-notorious-bergman.html 29 August 2019.

Rothman, William. *Notorious*. The Criterion Collection. 16 October 2001. Accessed online https:// www.criterion.com/current/posts/145-notorious 30 August 2019.

Schatz, Thomas. *Boom and Bust: American Cinema in the 1940s*. Berkeley: University of California Press, 1997.

Spoto, Donald. *The Dark Side of Genius: The Life of Alfred Hitchcock*. Boston: Little, Brown and Company, 1983.

Taylor, John Russell. *Hitch: The Life and Times of Alfred Hitchcock*. New York: Pantheon Books, 1978.

Torregrossa, Richard. *Cary Grant: A Celebration of Style*. New York: Bulfinch Press, 2006.

Truffaut, François. *Hitchcock*. New York: Simon & Schuster, 1983.

The Big Sleep

Bacall, Lauren. *By Myself*. New York: Alfred A. Knopf, 1979.

Benchley, Nathaniel. *Humphrey Bogart*. Boston: Little, Brown and Company, 1975.

Bogart, Stephen. *Bogart: In Search of My Father*. New York: Dutton, 1995.

Ebert, Roger. "The Big Sleep." RogerEbert.com. 22 June 1997. Accessed online 18 September 2019.

Hogan, David J. *Film Noir FAQ*. Milwaukee: Applause Theatre & Cinema Books, 2013.

Hyams, Joe. *Bogart & Bacall: A Love Story*. New York: David McKay Company, 1975.

Kanfer, Stefan. *Tough Without a Gun: The Life and Extraordinary Afterlife of Humphrey Bogart*. New York: Alfred A. Knopf, 2011.

Kobal, John. *People Will Talk*. New York: Alfred A. Knopf, 1986.

McCarthy, Todd. *Howard Hawks: The Grey Fox of Hollywood*. New York: Grove Press, 1997.

Parish, James Robert and Don E. Stanke. *The Forties Gals*. Westport, CT: Arlington, 1980.

Quirk, Lawrence J. *Lauren Bacall: Her Films and Career*. New York: The Citadel Press, 1986.

Schatz, Thomas. *Boom and Bust: American Cinema in the 1940s*. Berkeley: University of California Press, 1997.

Sperber, A.M. and Eric Lax. *Bogart*. New York: HarperCollins, 1997.

Taylor, Kerry. *Vintage Fashion and Couture: From Poiret to McQueen*. Buffalo, NY: Firefly Books, 2013.

The Killers

Dixon, Hugh. "Hollywood." *Pittsburgh Post Gazette*. 11 July 1946: 9. Print. Accessed at Newspapers. com 1 August 2019.

Jorgensen, Jay and Donald L. Scoggins. *Creating the Illusion: A Fashionable History of Hollywood Costume Designers*. Philadelphia: Running Press, 2015.

"Vera West, Designer, Takes Life Hinting at Blackmail." *Los Angeles Times*. 30 June 1947: 2. Print. Accessed at Newspapers.com 1 August 2019.

"Hollywood Seeks 'Realism' in Stars' Attire." *Santa Maria Times*. 28 September 1948: 3. Print. Accessed at Newspapers.com 1 August 2019.

MacEachern, James A. Mickey *Rooney: A Show Business Life*. Jefferson: McFarland & Company, 2017.

Schatz, Thomas. *Boom and Bust: American Cinema in the 1940s*. Berkeley: University of California Press, 1997.

Server, Lee. *Ava Gardner: "Love is Nothing."* New York: St. Martin's Griffin, 2006.

Vieira, Mark A. *Into the Dark: The Hidden World of Film Noir, 1941-1950*. Philadelphia: Running Press, 2016.

Wayne, Jane Ellen. *Ava's Men: The Private Life of Ava Gardner*. New York: St. Martin's Press. 1990.

Boom, Blacklist, and a New Look

"About GI Bill: History and Timeline." The Department of Veterans Affairs. 21 November 2013. Online. Accessed https://benefits.va.gov/gibill/history.asp 19 January 2020.

Amadeo, Kimberly. "Unemployment Rate by Year Since 1929 Compared to Inflation and GDP." The Balance. 3 January 2020. Accessed online https://www.thebalance.com/unemployment-rate-by-year-3305506 4 January 2020.

Angeletti, Norberto and Alberto Oliva. *In Vogue: The Illustrated History of the World's Most Famous Fashion Magazine*. New York: Rizzoli, 2006.

Barbieri, Annalisa. "When Skirts were Full and Women were Furious." *The Independent*. 3 March 1996. Online. Accessed https://www.independent.co.uk/news/when-skirts-were-full-and-women-were-furious-1340021.html 16 January 2020.

Bedwell, Bettina. "Movie Fashion Designers Must Be Good Prophets." *Daily News*. 22 September 1946. 67. Accessed Newspapers.com 21 November 2019.

Bond, David. *The Guinness Guide to 20th Century Fashion*. Enfield, Middlesex: Guinness Publishing, 1981.

Callahan, Eileen. "First Look at New Suits Shows Swing to Softness." *Daily News*. 8 August 1948. C10. Accessed Newspapers.com 27 November 2019.

Dixon, Wheeler Winston and Gwendolyn Audrey Foster. *A Short History of Film*. New Brunswick, NJ: Rutgers University Press, 2008.

Foley, Grace. "Irene Among Hollywood's Most Talented Designers." *The Ottawa Citizen*. 18 February 1948. 7. Accessed Newspapers.com 21 November 2019.

Friedrich, Otto. *City of Nets: A Portrait of Hollywood in the 1940s*. New York: Harper Perennial, 1986.

Grant, Linda. "Light at the End of the Tunnel." *The Guardian*. 21 September 2007. Online. Accessed https://www.theguardian.com/lifeandstyle/2007/sep/22/fashion.features 17 January 2020.

Head, Edith and Paddy Calistro. *Edith Head's Hollywood*. Santa Monica: Angel City Press, 2008.

Hennessy, Kathryn ed. *Fashion: The Definitive History of Costume and Style*. New York: Dorling Kindersley Limited, 2012.

Jorgensen, Jay. *Edith Head: The 50-Year Career of Hollywood's Greatest Costume Designer*. Philadelphia: Running Press, 2010.

Kelly, Emma. "Carmel Snow." The Costume Society. 25 May 2018. Online. Accessed http://costumesociety.org.uk/blog/post/carmel-snow 16 January 2020.

"Labor Force, Employment, and Unemployment, 1929-39: Estimating Methods." Bureau of Labor Statistics. Page 2, Table 1. Accessed online 3 January 2020 https://www.bls.gov/opub/mlr/1948/article/pdf/labor-force-employment-and-unemployment-1929-39-estimating-methods.pdf

Schatz, Thomas. *Boom and Bust: American Cinema in the 1940s*. Berkeley: University of California Press, 1997.

Sickels, Robert. *The 1940s*. Westport, CT: Greenwood Press, 2004.

Taylor, Kerry. *Vintage Fashion and Couture: From Poiret to McQueen*. Buffalo, NY: Firefly Books, 2013.

Uschan, Michael V. *The 1940s: A Cultural History of the United States Through the Decades*. San Diego: Lucent Books, 1999.

Walford, Jonathan. *Forties Fashion: From Siren Suits to the New Look*. New York: Thames & Hudson, 2008.

Winkler, Allan M. *Home Front U.S.A.: America During World War II*. Wheeling, WV: Harlan Davidson, 2012.

Dead Reckoning

Benchley, Nathaniel. *Humphrey Bogart*. Boston: Little, Brown and Company, 1975.

Bogart, Stephen. *Bogart: In Search of My Father*. New York: Dutton, 1995.

Colker, David. "Sultry Leading Lady of Film Noir." *Chicago Tribune*. 8 February 2015. Section 1 page 29. Accessed Newspapers.com 16 Dec 2019.

David, George L. "Bogart and Lizabeth Scott Score in Exciting Film at Loew's." *Rochester Democrat and Chronicle*. 21 February 1947. 16. Accessed Newspapers.com 14 Dec 2019.

De Klerk, Robbert (CEO of the Bogart Estate). Interview with the author, 4 December 2019.

Gliatto, Tom, Anne Marie Otey, Ulrica Wihlborg, and Nancy Matsumoto. "The Gift of Garb." *People*. 12 May 1997: 44-45. Print. Accessed at Margaret Herrick Library (AMPAS) 16 April 2015.

Hogan, David J. *Film Noir FAQ*. Milwaukee: Applause Theatre & Cinema Books, 2013.

Hopper, Hedda. "Repartee a la Mode." *Los Angeles Times*. 26 July 2019. Part II page 3. Accessed Newspapers.com 14 Dec 2019.

Hyams, Joe. *Bogart & Bacall: A Love Story*. New York: David McKay Company, 1975.

Jackson, Beverly. *Santa Barbara News Press*. 7 October 1990. Accessed at Margaret Herrick Library (AMPAS) 16 April 2005.

"Jean Louis." *People*. 9 February 1987: 76. Print. Accessed at Margaret Herrick Library (AMPAS) 16 April 2015.

"Jean Louis." *The Times* (London). 26 April 1997: unknown. Print. Accessed at Margaret Herrick Library (AMPAS) 16 April 2015.

"Jean Louis and His First Ladies." *W*. 27 March 1981: unknown. Print. Accessed at Margaret Herrick Library (AMPAS) 16 April 2015.

Johnson, Erskine. "Johnson's Hollywood." *The News-Herald*. 26 July 1946. 3. Accessed Newspapers. com 16 Dec 2019.

Jorgensen, Jay and Donald L. Scoggins. *Creating the Illusion: A Fashionable History of Hollywood Costume Designers*. Philadelphia: Running Press, 2015.

Kanfer, Stefan. *Tough Without a Gun: The Life and Extraordinary Afterlife of Humphrey Bogart*. New York: Alfred A. Knopf, 2011.

Kobal, John. *People Will Talk*. New York: Alfred A. Knopf, 1986.

Langer, Carole. Lizabeth Scott interview. 1996. 8 parts. Accessed YouTube 16 Dec 2019 https://www.youtube.com/user/soapbxprod/search?query=lizabeth+scott

Louis, Jean. Publicity interview on his career. Hollywood: Columbia Pictures, 20 July 1954. Print. Accessed at Margaret Herrick Library (AMPAS) 16 April 2015.

Modern Screen. January–June 1946: 8. Print. Accessed at Margaret Herrick Library (AMPAS) 16 April 2015.

Muller, Eddie. *Dark City: The Lost World of Film Noir*. New York: St. Martin's Griffin, 1998.

"Paris Fashions Transported by Movie Stylist." *The Valley Times*. 29 July 1946. 10. Accessed Newspapers.com 14 Dec 2019.

Schneider, Sven Raphael. "The Caraceni Dynasty Explained." *Gentleman's Gazette*. 26 September 2011. Online. https://www.gentlemansgazette.com/caraceni-domenico-bespoke-tailor-rome/ Accessed 18 December 2019.

Silver, Alain and Elizabeth Ward eds. *Film Noir: An Encyclopedic Reference to the American Style*. Woodstock, NY: The Overlook Press, 1980.

"Society-Women's Interests-Health and the Home." *Honolulu Star-Bulletin*. 24 March 1947. 13. Accessed Newspapers.com 14 Dec 2019.

Sperber, A.M. and Eric Lax. *Bogart*. New York: HarperCollins, 1997.

Stack, Rosemarie. "Natural Elegance." *Movieline*. 25 July 1986: unknown. Accessed at Margaret Herrick Library (AMPAS) 16 April 2015.

Vallance, Tom. "Obituary: Jean Louis." *The Independent*. 25 April 1997. Online. Accessed https://www.independent.co.uk/news/obituaries/obituary-jean-louis-1269135.html 27 July 2019.

Weil, Martin. "Lizabeth Scott: 'The Queen of Film Noir' Who Played the Femme Fatale Opposite Bogart, Mitchum, Douglas, Lancaster, and Powell." *The Independent*. 10 February 2015. Accessed https://www.independent.co.uk/news/people/news/lizabeth-scott-the-queen-of-film-noir-who-played-the-femme-fatale-opposite-bogart-mitchum-douglas-10037044.html 17 December 2019.

Lady in the Lake

Billecci, Frank and Lauranne B. Fisher. *Irene: A Designer from the Golden Age of Hollywood: The MGM Years 1942-1949*. Atglen, PA: Schiffer Publishing, 2013.

Bird, David. "Robert Montgomery, Actor, Dies at 77." *The New York Times*. 28 September 1981. B-6. https://www.nytimes.com/1981/09/28/obituaries/robert-montgomery-actor-dies-at-77.html Accessed 23 November 2019.

Eames, John Douglas. *The MGM Story*. New York: Crown Publishers Inc., 1976.

Foley, Grace. "'Irene' Among Hollywood's Most Talented Designers." *The Evening Citizen*. 18 February 1948. 7. Accessed Newspapers.com 23 Nov 2019.

Friedrich, Otto. *City of Nets: A Portrait of Hollywood in the 1940s*. New York: Harper Perennial, 1980.

Hopper, Hedda. "Hollywood." *The Daily News*. 25 November 1946. C12. Accessed Newspapers.com 23 Nov 2019.

Jorgensen, Jay and Donald L. Scoggins. *Creating the Illusion: A Fashionable History of Hollywood Costume Designers*. Philadelphia: Running Press, 2015.

McClelland, Doug. *Forties Film Talk: Oral Histories of Hollywood*. Jefferson: McFarland & Company, 1992.

Milano, Nicole. "Hollywood Movie Star Robert Montgomery, June 1940." *American Field Service*. 1 October 2012. https://afs.org/2012/10/01/hollywood-movie-star-robert-montgomery-june-1940/ Accessed 23 November 2019.

"Mission Accomplished." *The Kenosha Evening News*. 11 July 1946. 17. Accessed Newspapers.com 23 November 2019.

Muller, Eddie. *Dark City Dames: The Wicked Women of Film Noir*. New York: ReganBooks, 2001.

Muller, Eddie. *Dark City: The Lost World of Film Noir*. New York: St. Martin's Griffin, 1998.

Perry, Phyllis. "That Old 'New Look.'" *The Salt Lake Tribune*. 7 December 1947. D3. Accessed Newspapers.com 23 Nov 2019

"Robert Montgomery." SAG-AFTRA. https://www.sagaftra.org/robert-montgomery Accessed 23 November 2019.

Schallert, Edwin. "Brilliant Screen Career Dawns for Audrey Totter." *Los Angeles Times*. 2 February 1947. Part III 2. Accessed Newspapers.com 23 November 2019.

Schallert, Edwin. "Lady in Lake Intriguing." *Los Angeles Times*. 15 February 1947. Part II 5. Accessed Newspapers.com 23 November 2019.

Seeger, Rea. "Irene Dictates Styles Stars Wear in Films." *Chicago Daily Tribune*. 20 September 1946. 24. Accessed Newspapers.com 23 Nov 2019.

Silver, Alain and Elizabeth Ward, eds. *Film Noir: An Encyclopedic Reference to the American Style*. New York: The Overlook Press, 1980.

Sher, Jack. "How to Win an Argument." *Los Angeles Times*. 2 March 1947. Accessed Newspapers.com 23 November 2019.

Snead, Elizabeth. "The Chic Life and Tragic Death of a Revered Costume Designer." *The Hollywood Reporter*. 29 March 2013. Accessed https://www.hollywoodreporter.com/news/irene-lentz-costume-designers-chic-430898 25 November 2019

Out of the Past

"Fountain's Presents Stevenson-Designed Bridal Ensembles." *Greenwood Commonwealth*. 21 November 1947. 3. Accessed Newspapers.com 6 Nov 2019.

Graham, Sheilah. "Jane Greer's Smile Means Much to Her." *The Indianapolis Star*. 18 May 1947. Accessed Newspapers.com 6 December 2019.

Greer, Jane. "TCM Word of Mouth: Jane Greer on Out of the Past." Turner Classic Movies. Interstitial. August 1997. Accessed online https://twitter.com/tcm/status/1042093392174440449 9 December 2019.

Hampton, Mary. "Clothes Should Glorify Wearer, Says Designer." *The Californian*. 31 March 1 April 1938. 14. Accessed Newspapers.com 7 Dec 2019.

Hart, Alicia. "Glorifying Yourself: Jewelry Needs Plain Background." *The Fresno Bee*. 7 July 1945. 5. Accessed at Newspapers.com 25 October 2019.

Hogan, David J. *Film Noir FAQ*. Milwaukee: Applause Theatre & Cinema Books, 2013.

Jones, Will. "Crosby—Minus Singing Voice." *Minneapolis Morning Tribune*. 29 December 1947. 14. Accessed Newspapers.com 6 December 2019.

Jorgensen, Jay and Donald L. Scoggins. *Creating the Illusion: A Fashionable History of Hollywood Costume Designers*. Philadelphia: Running Press, 2015.

McClelland, Doug. *Forties Film Talk: Oral Histories of Hollywood*. Jefferson: McFarland & Company, 1992.

McKeon, Shiela. "What Women are Doing: Beauty Secret." *Brooklyn Eagle*. 14 July 1947. 2. Accessed Newspapers.com 6 December 2019.

Muller, Eddie. *Dark City: The Lost World of Film Noir*. New York: St. Martin's Press, 1998.

"Out of the Past is Film of Murder and Desire." *The Indianapolis News*. 30 January 1948. 10. Accessed Newspapers.com 6 December 2019.

Schallert, Edwin. "Woman Puts Jane Greer on Ladder to Film Fame." *Los Angeles Times*. 16 February 1947. 1-2. Accessed Newspapers.com 6 December 2019.

Schatz, Thomas. *Boom and Bust: American Cinema in the 1940s*. Berkeley: University of California Press, 1997.

Vieira, Mark A. *Into the Dark: The Hidden World of Film Noir*, 1941-1950. Philadelphia: Running Press, 2016.

Weaver, Sylva. "East and West Struggle for Fashion Dictatorship." *Los Angeles Times*. 19 February 1941. 13. Accessed Newspapers.com 6 December 2019.

Whittemore, Hank. "My Life in Hollywood's Golden Age." *The Lincoln Star, Parade Magazine*. 20 February 1994. 14-15. Accessed at Newspapers.com 25 October 2019.

The Lady from Shanghai

Callahan, Eileen. "Dress Interest Concentrated Above Waist in New Fashions." *The Daily News*. 14 August 1948. 16. Accessed Newspapers.com 27 Nov 2019.

Callahan, Eileen. "Dress-like Coat Makes Style News on the Beach." *The Daily News*. 13 August 1948. C14. Accessed Newspapers.com 27 Nov 2019.

Callahan, Eileen. "Fashion Softens Severe Lines to Avoid Angular Silhouettes." *The Daily News*. 13 September 1948. 42. Accessed Newspapers.com 30 November 2019.

Callahan, Eileen. "First Look at New Suits Show Swing to Softness." *The Daily News*. 8 August 1948. C10. Accessed Newspapers.com 27 Nov 2019.

Callahan, Eileen. "Gowns That are Remembered are Real Beauty Composite." *The Daily News*. 28 August 1948. 16. Accessed Newspapers.com 27 Nov 2019.

Callahan, Eileen. "Hollywood Designer Predicts Black and White Beachwear." *The Daily News*. 7 August 1948. C12. Accessed Newspapers.com 27 Nov 2019.

Callow, Simon. *Orson Welles Volume 2: Hello Americans*. New York: Penguin Books, 2006.

Gliatto, Tom, Anne Marie Otey, Ulrica Wihlborg, and Nancy Matsumoto. "The Gift of Garb." *People*. 12 May 1997: 44-45. Print. Accessed at Margaret Herrick Library (AMPAS) 16 April 2015.

Hallowell, John. "Rita Hayworth is Still Alive But Out of Work." *Los Angeles Times*. 30 June 1968. 22-F. Accessed 29 November 2019.

Hogan, David J. *Film Noir FAQ*. Milwaukee: Applause Theatre & Cinema Books, 2013.

Jackson, Beverly. *Santa Barbara News Press*. 7 October 1990. Accessed at Margaret Herrick Library (AMPAS) 16 April 2005.

Jean Louis. Publicity interview on his career. Hollywood: Columbia Pictures, 20 July 1954. Print. Accessed at Margaret Herrick Library (AMPAS) 16 April 2015.

"Jean Louis." *People*. 9 February 1987: 76. Print. Accessed at Margaret Herrick Library (AMPAS) 16 April 2015.

"Jean Louis." *The Times* (London). 26 April 1997: unknown. Print. Accessed at Margaret Herrick Library (AMPAS) 16 April 2015.

"Jean Louis and His First Ladies." *W*. 27 March 1981: unknown. Print. Accessed at Margaret Herrick Library (AMPAS) 16 April 2015.

Johnson, Erskine. "In Hollywood." *Miami Daily News*. 12 May 1948. 8. Accessed Newspapers.com 29 November 2019.

Jorgensen, Jay and Donald L. Scoggins. *Creating the Illusion: A Fashionable History of Hollywood Costume Designers*. Philadelphia: Running Press, 2015.

Kobal, John. *People Will Talk*. New York: Alfred A. Knopf, 1986.

"Lady from Shanghai Stars Rita Hayworth." *The Kingsport Times-News*. 25 July 1948. 25. Accessed Newspapers.com 29 November 2019.

Leaming, Barbara. *If This Was Happiness: A Biography of Rita Hayworth*. New York: Viking Penguin,

1989.

Leaming, Barbara. *Orson Welles: A Biography*. New York: First Limelight Edition, 1985.

Louis, Jean. Publicity interview on his career. Hollywood: Columbia Pictures, 20 July 1954. Print. Accessed at Margaret Herrick Library (AMPAS) 16 April 2015.

Modern Screen. January–June 1946: 8. Print. Accessed at Margaret Herrick Library (AMPAS) 16 April 2015.

"Rita Hayworth Not Redheaded." *The Daily Press*. 17 November 1946. 48. Accessed Newspapers. com 29 November 2019.

Ringgold, Gene. *The Films of Rita Hayworth: The Legend & Career of a Love Goddess*. Secaucus: The Citadel Press, 1974.

Sanders, James R. "Rita Hayworth." *Vogue Italia*. 9 August 2012. Online. Accessed https://www. vogue.it/en/vogue-curvy/glam-and-curvy/2012/08/rita-hayworth 27 July 2019.

Silver, Alain and Elizabeth Ward eds. *Film Noir: An Encyclopedic Reference to the American Style*. Woodstock, NY: The Overlook Press, 1980.

Stack, Rosemarie. "Natural Elegance." *Movieline*. 25 July 1986: unknown. Accessed at Margaret Herrick Library (AMPAS) 16 April 2015.

Terry, Dickson. "Rita Hayworth's Ambulating Romance with Son of the Fabulous Aga Khan has Whole World Talking—Colossal is Only Word to Describe It." *St. Louis Post-Dispatch*. 16 January 1949. 1G. Accessed Newspapers.com 29 November 2019.

Vallance, Tom. "Obituary: Jean Louis." *The Independent*. 25 April 1997. Online. Accessed https:// www.independent.co.uk/news/obituaries/obituary-jean-louis-1269135.html 27 July 2019.

Welles, Orson. The Lady from Shanghai. Screenplay (final draft for estimating purposes). 17 August 1946. https://www.scribd.com/document/286846150/The-Lady-From-Shanghai-1947-Draft-Script

Welles, Orson and Peter Bogdanovich. *This is Orson Welles*. New York: Da Capo Press, 1992.

The Asphalt Jungle

Burnett, W. R. *The Asphalt Jungle*. London: Prion Books Limited, 1999 (first published 1949). Downloaded e-book from GoodReads.com. 19 October 2019.

Grobel, Lawrence. *The Hustons*. New York: Charles Scribner's Sons, 1989.

Heffernan, Harold. "Marilyn Monroe Stages Comeback—At 21." *The Pittsburgh Press*. 18 June 1950. Accessed through Newspapers.com 16 October 2019.

Hogan, David J. *Film Noir FAQ*. Milwaukee: Applause Theatre & Cinema Books, 2013.

Huston, John. *An Open Book*. New York: Alfred A Knopf, 1980.

Jorgensen, Jay and Donald L. Scoggins. *Creating the Illusion: A Fashionable History of Hollywood Costume Designers*. Philadelphia: Running Press, 2015.

Lane, Lydia. "Marilyn Monroe Gives Her Ideas on Beauty." *The Marshall News Messenger*. 28 December 1952. Accessed via Newspapers.com 16 October 2019.

Muller, Eddie. *Dark City: The Lost World of Film Noir*. New York: St. Martin's Griffin, 1998.

Rose, Helen. *Just Make Them Beautiful*. Santa Monica: Dennis-Landman, 1976.

Spoto, Donald. *Marilyn Monroe: The Biography*. New York: Cooper Square Press, 1993.

Strumme, Jorjett (former assistant to Helen Rose). Interview by email, 14 February 2019.

Sunset Boulevard

DeMille, Cecil B. *The Autobiography of Cecil B. DeMille*. New Jersey: Prentice-Hall, Inc., 1959.

Head, Edith and Paddy Calistro. *Edith Head's Hollywood*. Santa Monica: Angel City Press, 2008.

Jorgensen, Jay and Donald L. Scoggins. *Creating the Illusion: A Fashionable History of Hollywood Costume Designers*. Philadelphia: Running Press, 2015.

Jorgensen, Jay. *Edith Head: The 50-Year Career of Hollywood's Greatest Costume Designer*. Philadelphia: Running Press, 2010.

Leese, Elizabeth. *Costume Design in the Movies*. New York: Dover Publications, 1991.

Presley, Cecilia DeMille and Mark A. Vieira. *Cecil B. DeMille: The Art of the Hollywood Epic*. Philadelphia: Running Press, 2014.

Shearer, Stephen Michael. *Gloria Swanson: The Ultimate Star*. New York: St. Martin's Press, 2013.

Acknowledgments

My first book was a long time coming and it's only fitting that I began with 1940s film noir. My father, a career police officer who preferred the graveyard shift for its dark drama, would come home in the middle of the night and watch noir like *The Maltese Falcon* and *The Big Sleep* to unwind after work. That was the beginning of my love for classic film.

My mother, a career librarian, supported my love of reading and research. One of the benefits of her job was that she would bring home piles of books from authors like Dashiell Hammett for us to read. I spent many hours poring over the pages of crime fiction growing up. She has continued to support my research by sending me classic film biographies. Many were referenced for this book.

Her mother, Genevieve, my fiercely independent grandmother, believed I was destined for great things. She supported me through times when no one else did. I would not be here today if not for her and honor her memory with this book.

Film Noir Style came to fruition largely because of the support of Jeff Mantor. Head of Hollywood's legendary Larry Edmunds Bookshop, Jeff is the patron saint of film historians for his tireless work on our behalf. He long believed I should write a book, and I could not appreciate him more. Many thanks to my GoodKnight Books publisher and editor Mary Rothhaar for taking a chance on a first-time author and offering me valuable feedback. I also thank fellow GKB author Robert Matzen for his empathy and support through the entire project. Smith Publicity's Sarah Miniaci was behind the book from the beginning and helped get the word out even as the world was changing around us. Another invaluable collaborator was Alison Jo Rigney, who empowered me with wonderful images from the Everett Collection for this book and other projects.

My thanks also to John McElwee of Greenbriar Picture Shows for providing several images that appear in this book. And the whole look of *Film Noir Style* came together because of designer Sharon Berk with an assist from Valerie Sloan, who perfected some of the images.

There are historians and authors I turn to again and again as trusted sources. First and foremost, I thank my friend and colleague Eddie Muller. Few know the dark world of noir better. He has done so much to preserve its history and promote its legacy, especially with the Film Noir Foundation and Noir City film festivals. You will see him quoted several times in *Film Noir Style*, referencing our own conversations as well as two of his books. Another is Jay Jorgensen who shares my passion for shining a light on the lives of Hollywood costume designers. Along with David Chierichetti, he has done an incredible amount of research in order to share their stories. Of course I utilized the insights of many authors for *Film Noir Style* and they are all mentioned in the Chapter Notes.

I was fortunate to be able to go straight to archivists for information on many of the costumes and jewelry featured in this book. Thanks in particular to Paramount's Randall Thropp for his friendship and access to that studio's archive, which exists because of his vision, passion, and protection. Thanks as well to Kristen and Tina Joseff for providing me ongoing access to their archive and the history of Joseff of Hollywood. Stephanie Lake, caretaker of the Bonnie Cashin archive, provided me with a lovely portrait of the costume designer for *Film Noir Style*. And much appreciation goes to everyone at the Margaret Herrick Library for their invaluable resources.

To members of my classic film family—you know who you are—I cannot thank you enough. Many of you have supported me from the very beginning of this journey, and you have given me strength all along the way. I appreciate you every day.

And last, but absolutely not least, the person to whom this book is dedicated—Kevin Osborne. He also adores classic film, and our relationship began almost three decades ago with a triple feature of *Rear Window*, *Manhattan*, and *La Dolce Vita*. That summer weekend was also where I discovered my vocation in film and fashion history. Kevin is unrivaled for his belief in me and has stood by my side even in the toughest of times. He loves noir and its style as much as I do, and I believe this book is a fitting tribute to him.

Index